IRELAND'S SUFFRAGETTES

IRELAND'S SUFFRAGETTES

The Women who Fought for the Vote

SARAH-BETH WATKINS

First published 2014

The History Press Ireland
50 City Quay
Dublin 2
Ireland
www.thehistorypress.ie

© Sarah-Beth Watkins, 2014

The right of Sarah-Beth Watkins to be identified as the Author
of this work has been asserted in accordance with the
Copyright, Designs and Patents Act 1988.

All rights reserved. No part of this book may be reprinted
or reproduced or utilised in any form or by any electronic,
mechanical or other means, now known or hereafter invented,
including photocopying and recording, or in any information
storage or retrieval system, without the permission in writing
from the Publishers.

British Library Cataloguing in Publication Data.
A catalogue record for this book is available from the British Library.

ISBN 978 1 84588 824 4

Typesetting and origination by The History Press

Contents

Abbreviations	6
Acknowledgements	7
Introduction	9

The Militant Suffragettes — 17

Margaret Connery	17
Margaret Cousins	20
Kathleen Emerson	25
Mabel Purser	30
Hanna Sheehy Skeffington	32
Marguerite Palmer	38
The Murphy Sisters	41
Barbara Hoskins	45
Kathleen Houston	46

The English Suffragettes — 48

Mary Leigh	49
Lizzie Baker	49
Gladys Evans	50

The Belfast Suffragettes — 54

The Political Suffragettes — 58

Anna Haslam	58
Louie Bennett	62
Charlotte Despard	67
Maude Gonne	70
Eva Gore-Booth	75
Mary Hayden	80
Rosamund Jacob	82
Delia Larkin	85
Countess Constance de Markievicz	89
Somerville and Ross	95
Isabella Tod	98
Jennie Wyse Power	101
Kathleen Lynn	108
Mary Colum	112
Marion Duggan	115
Mary MacSwiney	119
Susanne Rouviere Day	123
Helen Chenevix	126
Dora Mellone	129
Margaret McCoubrey	133

Afterword	137
Notes	139
Bibliography	143

Abbreviations

DWSA	Dublin Women's Suffrage Association
ITGWU	Irish Transport and General Workers' Union
IWF	Irish Women's Franchise League
IWRL	Irish Women's Reform League
IWSF	Irish Women's Suffrage Federation
IWSLGA	Irish Women's Suffrage and Local Government Association
IWSS	Irish Women's Suffrage Society
IWWU	Irish Women Workers' Union
MWFL	Munster Women's Franchise League
NESWS	North of England Society for Women's Suffrage
WILPF	Women's International League for Peace and Freedom
WSPU	Women's Social and Political Union

Acknowledgements

I would like to thank all those who have helped in my research during the course of writing this book, including the staff of the National Archives and the National Library in Dublin for their kind assistance and the answering of many queries, as well as the staff of the Museum of London and the British Library. In particular, I would like to thank the British Library for permission to quote Kathleen Emerson's poems from 'Holloway Jingles', a Women's Social and Political Union pamphlet compiled by N.A. John.

I would also like to thank the National Archives of Ireland and its director for kind permission to quote from their archived sources and the National Library of Ireland and the Museum of London for permission to reproduce photographic material.

Many thanks also go to Simon and Jill Muggleton for information on their ancestors, the Murphy/Cadiz sisters, and to Elizabeth Crawford, Sandra McAvoy, Una Lawlor and Elizabeth Kyte for helping to point me in the right direction with my research.

Kind regards also go to Dr Louise Ryan for allowing me permission to reproduce paragraphs from the *Irish Citizen* newspaper taken from her book, *Irish Feminism and the Vote*.

Last but not least I would like to thank my family for giving me the space and time to mull over my research and for listening to me when I was ranting on about suffragettes!

Introduction

Ireland's Suffragettes is a collection of biographical essays on the main suffragettes who influenced Ireland's struggle for women's rights. Many of the women were political activists while others became militant suffragettes between 1912 and 1914. Irish suffragettes were imprisoned for their beliefs in Ireland and the UK as well as being involved in movements across the world, like Margaret Cousins who began her campaign for suffrage in Ireland and continued the fight for women's rights in India.

The suffrage movement in Ireland began in the late 1800s and the first public meeting was held in Dublin in 1870. It was then that women like Anna Haslam and Isabella Tod began to debate what they could do to obtain the vote for the women of Ireland. Up until this time, women had been treated as second-class citizens with barely any rights. They were not allowed to hold public office or vote in parliamentary elections, access to education was limited and they lost the right to own property on marriage, with any assets given to their husbands. Women could be forced to hand over any wages to their husbands and they had no rights where their children were concerned. It was a patriarchal society and it was an unequal world for women. They felt that the time was ripe for change.

The first Irish suffrage organisation, the Dublin Women's Suffrage Association (DWSA), was established in 1876 and it began a process of women working collectively across Ireland towards their aims. In 1898, women were allowed to sit on Rural and Urban District Councils and Town Commissions, but not on County Councils or Borough Councils. In the following elections, over 100 women were elected to these seats. Women had realised that the route to change was through their involvement in politics and this could only occur through having the right to vote.

Suffrage organisations began to spring up, with women getting together across the country to mobilise for access to greater equality. In 1908, the Irish Women's Franchise League (IWFL) was founded and 1911 saw the Irish Women's Suffrage Federation (IWSF) and the Irish Women Workers' Union (IWWU) established. Between 1912 and 1914, the suffrage movement in Ireland was at its peak. In November 1912, seventy-one members of the Irish Parliamentary Party voted against the Women's Suffrage Bill and Women's Suffrage Amendments to the Home Rule Bill. The women were furious and decided, for the first time, that constitutional methods for obtaining the vote were not enough. During this two-year period, all the militant action took place and the movement gained publicity and support. But Ireland was a country in turmoil and the political situation was one that the suffragettes fiercely debated, taking sides and arguing over what their priorities were.

Cumann na mBan was founded in 1914 and the Easter Rising occurred in 1916. These were troubled years in Irish history and many of the suffragettes were caught up in the nationalist cause. The struggle of the suffragettes in Ireland was different in that respect to that of the UK;

Extension of Franchise poster. (© National Library of Ireland) many Irish suffragettes were also included in the struggle for independence and the inclusion of women in the trade union movement. Loyalties were divided and the dispute and discussion that ensued was often played out in the pages of the *Irish Citizen*, the suffrage newspaper. Today, this newspaper gives us a true testimony of the facts and opinions of the women involved in the suffrage movement, and lets us examine their relationship to nationalism, the labour movement, and each other.

The fight for votes for women in Ireland was not easy. Many people were against women's suffrage, feeling they had no place in the political environment and that women would complicate matters if they were more involved in the politics of Ireland. Some nationalists agreed women should have the vote, but only if Ireland was a Free State. The Labour movement supported the right to vote but unionists didn't. This was all complicated by the relationship Ireland had to Britain. For the suffragettes who had often travelled to the UK to attend meetings of the Women's Social and Political Union (WSPU), this was never more apparent than when English suffragettes came to Dublin and acted without their knowledge. Many denounced the women and their attack on Prime Minister Asquith but others supported them, especially when they were force-fed in an Irish prison. In contrast, suffragettes in Ulster welcomed their English counterparts when they wanted to take part in more direct militant action and agreed to the WSPU's involvement in the North. The suffrage situation in Ireland became extremely complicated, but through it all women worked diligently to obtain the right to vote and what they felt would be a turning point in women's equality with men.

In 1918, women were allowed to vote for the first time but with conditions. They had to be over 30 and own

The *Irish Citizen* newspaper. (© National Library of Ireland) property or satisfy other qualifications. As we shall see in her biography, Countess de Markievicz was the first woman to be elected to Dail Éireann. The right to vote was finally granted in 1922 when all men and women in the Irish Free State over the age of 21 were allowed to vote, six years before the same right was granted to the women of Britain. For all the complications of the Irish suffrage movement, the women had prevailed.

The centenary of the last conviction of a suffragette in an Irish court will be in 2014. The suffragette movement was interrupted by the First World War when many of the women became involved in other activities: some supporting the war effort, others working for peace. Militant action ceased and did not continue after the war, although many of the women were still involved in the movement.

Drawing on primary sources, *Ireland's Suffragettes* brings to life not only the most famous names in the suffragette movement, but also the other women who made women's rights their life's work. The women came from many different backgrounds and each one has a story to tell. For ease of reading, this book is split into two parts: the militant suffragettes and the political ones. The militant suffragettes are the women who were convicted and imprisoned, whilst the political focus on women who used more constitutional methods, but many of the women were both. Some started off hoping that reform would come about by lobbying MPs and gathering public support but when this failed to materialise, the women felt that they had no alternative but to take more direct action to highlight their cause and force politicians to take note. Some of the names will be familiar to you while others, I hope, will be women that you have not heard of before. All of them made voting a possibility for women today.

NB: The terms suffragist and suffragette have been used interchangeably throughout the text. We have come to use the term suffragette to encompass all the women who fought for the right to vote within the suffrage movement but at the time, a suffragette was a radical, militant member of the movement, whereas a suffragist was anyone involved in the fight for the right to vote.

The Militant Suffragettes

Margaret Connery
(1887–?)

Margaret was born in 1887 in Westport, County Mayo and was known as Meg to her friends. Very little is known about her early life but she was one of the most active and militant suffragettes. Meg was living in Dublin at a boarding house on Rathmines Road owned by Sarah Bateman in 1912 at the time when the suffrage movement took a more aggressive approach. She was vice-chairwoman of the IWFL, the most radical of the Irish suffrage groups.

Meg was on the speaker's platform when Prime Minister Asquith visited Dublin and was subsequently caught up in the disorder that followed where suffragettes were heckled by members of the Ancient Order of Hibernians. On the 6 November 1912, Meg was smashing windows at the Custom House on Dublin Quays with Kathleen Emerson. Arrested by Constable McQuaid, they were taken to Store Street police station. In court the next day, the women refused to pay their fine and were detained in Mountjoy Prison on 18 November.

The *Daily Express* noted that other suffragette action had occurred that night, although no one was arrested or prosecuted for it. Pillar-boxes in Lower Baggot Street, Merrion Square, Clare Street, and around the Pembroke and Ballsbridge districts of Dublin were filled with a corrosive liquid, ink and oil that damaged letters. On each of the pillar boxes, a note was left that read 'Votes for Women'. Had Meg and Kathleen been active all night or were they aided by other suffragettes?

On her incarceration, Meg immediately wrote to the chairman of the General Prisons Board stating, 'I have been imprisoned today for refusing to pay fine imposed for breaking Gov glass as a suffragist protest & am being treated as an ordinary criminal. I wish to have the question of prison treatment raised at once'.[1]

Margaret Cousins, the secretary of the IWFL, wrote to the Lord Lieutenant in Dublin Castle to draw his attention to the women being treated as common criminals, including Meg, pointing out that suffragettes were political prisoners which gave them certain privileges. J.B. Dougherty, writing on behalf of the Lord Lieutenant, did not agree to Margaret's demands. He replied that 'imprisonment was not an integral part of the sentence, but would follow necessarily upon failure to pay the damages and fines imposed by the court. Payment would avoid imprisonment, and in those circumstances His Excellency is not empowered to interfere with the course of the Law.' Both letters were published in *The Irish Times*, but by this time the women had been released.

Meg's prison notes also mention that she had served seven days in Holloway for damage done as a suffragette and she is mentioned in a list published in the *Irish Citizen* of the Irish suffragettes that had been imprisoned in the UK. She was still fighting for women's suffrage in January of 1913, when she was arrested for breaking more government windows with Margaret Cousins, Barbara Hoskins and Mabel

Purser. This time, Meg was sent to serve out her sentence in Tullamore Prison. Again the women asked to be treated as political prisoners or first-class misdemeanants. This was not granted, but they were still allowed their own clothes, to talk, write and exercise. However, the women would not back down from their request and began a hunger strike on 3 February until they were given more privileges. They began to eat again six days later and were not forcibly fed. Meg was released on 27 February with Margaret Cousins.

In November of 1913, Edward Carson, the Ulster Unionist leader and Andrew Bonar Law, leader of the Conservative Party, were in Dublin to give speeches on the Home Rule situation. As they were leaving the meeting to visit Lord Iveagh, Meg and Hanna Sheehy Skeffington broke through the police cordon and tried to press their pamphlets in his hands. They wanted to protest against the fact that no female delegates were allowed at these closed talks and that Bonar Law had refused to meet with the suffragettes. They were both arrested and charged with obstructing the police.

In 1914, Meg set off to bring the suffrage movement to Longford, Carrick-on-Shannon and Boyle. The north-west of Ireland was long seen as a black hole by the suffragists, with no groups or societies working for the cause. Hanna Sheehy Skeffington accompanied Meg and the tour was successful, bringing new converts into the movement.

In 1918, Meg chaired the conference of Cumann na dTeachtaire, an organisation set up to monitor the political environment in respect of women's interests and to make sure that women's issues were brought to the attention of the appropriate politicians. The conference was held to discuss the issue of venereal disease and Regulation 40 D of the Defence of the Realm Act (DORA) that aimed to protect soldiers from infection. In reality, this meant that any woman could be arrested and subjected to a medical examination.

The suffrage movement was outraged by this attack on women's rights and fought for the act to be abolished.

Throughout Meg's involvement in the suffrage movement and her tenure as a member of the IWFL, Meg wrote for the *Irish Citizen*. She wrote on topics such as 'Irish Militants, the War and Relief Work', 'Women and Labour' and 'Morality – Conventional or Otherwise'. In one of her last articles, 'The New Force in Irish Politics', published in August 1918, Meg said:

> If the new woman voter in Ireland has the courage and independence to set a new standard I believe the men of the new generation would try hard to live up to it. There are some questions of burning interest to women which men, even the best of them, will obstinately refuse to face or to think out, unless and until women compel them to face them … Will Irishwomen set a new standard for their country? Will they pierce through the froth of politics to the eternal verities beneath? Irishwomen have a long-inherited passion for national liberty. They will ring through on that issue. May they be equally true and uncompromising on the deep human issues …[2]

Margaret Cousins
(1878–1954)

Margaret Cousins was born Margaret Elizabeth Gillespie in 1878 in Boyle, County Roscommon to a Protestant family. Her father, Joseph, worked as a clerk in the courthouse in the town. Margaret spent her early life in Boyle attending its national school but moved to Dublin in 1898 to study music in the Royal Irish Academy. Margaret graduated with a degree in music from the Academy in 1902 and went on to teach music on a part-time basis in Dublin.

Margaret married James Cousins in Sandymount in 1903. James was a poet and critic who frequented Dublin's literary circle and later co-edited the *Irish Citizen*. They became friends with some of literatures greatest writers, including W.B. Yeats, James Joyce and George Russell. They were both vegetarians, interested in the temperance movement, anti-vivisection, socialism and later, the theosophical society.

In 1906, Margaret joined the Irish Women's Suffrage and Local Government Association (IWSLGA) but she quickly became unhappy with their pacifist stance. She co-founded the IWFL in 1908 with Hanna Sheehy Skeffington to form a more militant organisation. In James and Margaret's autobiography she says, 'Hannah asked us and some other friends to join in working out a scheme for a militant suffrage society suitable to the different political situation of Ireland'.[1] The IWFL aimed to use both peaceful and forceful methods to obtain the vote for women on the same grounds as Irish men, yet be non-party and open to all Irish women regardless of their affiliations. Margaret explained in her autobiography:

> We were as keen as men on the freedom of Ireland, but we saw the men clamouring for amendments which suited their own interests, and made no recognition of the existence of women as fellow citizens. We women were convinced that anything which improved the status of women would improve, not hinder, the coming of real national self-government.[2]

The IWFL was modelled on the WSPU and Margaret spent three weeks with them in 1909, learning tactics to use in the suffrage struggle in Ireland. Margaret was then invited to the UK by Mrs Pankhurst to attend the Parliament of Women in Caxton Hall which ended in a mass protest. The 18 November 1910 became known as 'Black Friday' when over 300 women, including Margaret, marched on the House of Commons when they found out that Prime Minister Asquith had no intention of giving the vote to women.

Black Friday, London, 1910. (© Museum of London)

The women were assaulted by the police, being beaten, punched, kicked and thrown to the ground. This was the first case of documented police abuse against the suffragettes and the press leapt to their defence amidst rumours that the women had also been sexually assaulted.

A few days later, as the protest and militant action continued, Margaret was smashing the windows of Cabinet Ministers' houses in Downing Street with potatoes and flowerpots for which she was sentenced to a month's imprisonment in Holloway Jail.

During 1911–1912, Margaret was back at home and she spent the time touring the country, bringing the suffrage message to women across Ireland with several other campaigners. But public speaking didn't come easy to Margaret and she admitted that she rehearsed 'in a field behind our house with only an ass for my audience'.[3] It was only a matter of time before she was caught up in more militant action as their pleas for suffrage continued to be ignored.

On 28 January 1913, Margaret was one of several women who broke windows at Dublin Castle. She was sentenced to a month's imprisonment in Tullamore Prison with Margaret Connery, Barbara Hoskins and Mabel Purser, where she went on hunger strike until the women were treated as political prisoners. In a letter to the chairman of the Prison Board, Margaret wrote, 'I am not a criminal but a political prisoner – my motives were neither criminal nor personal – being wholly associated with the agitation to obtain Votes for Women. I shall fight in every way in my power against being branded a criminal'.[4] Although they were not officially recognised as political prisoners, the women were all allowed daily visits, to be able to write letters, to have their own food and were exempted from hard labour. The women stopped their hunger strike on 8 February and Margaret was released on the 27th of the same month. In records pertaining to their incarceration, it is noted that there had been no forcible feeding.

The next day, an article that Margaret had written appeared in the *Irish Independent* entitled 'In Tullamore

Dublin Castle. (© National Library of Ireland)

Jail – A Prisoner's Story'. It detailed life in Tullamore for the prisoners and their experiences. In it, she says:

> We were fighting for our own personal honour, for the continuance of political treatment for all future reformers who might like ourselves break the law in order to amend the law, and for sex equality in political treatment as in everything else. Our weapons were determination, the power of mind over matter, faith in the victory of Right, and sacrifice of our appetites, and if need be even of our bodies, rather than that Wrong should prevail.

At the end of the article she sounds even more determined to carry on the fight for women's suffrage:

> ... I and my comrades have come out of prison rested in body, refreshed in mind, inspired in soul, with greater contempt than ever for the present Government and its despicable policy, and greater determination than ever to fight the battle of Woman Suffrage to a victorious end, as we did the Battle of Tullamore.[5]

Amongst the women who were convicted in Ireland for suffragette action were some members of the WSPU, namely Mary Leigh and Gladys Evan. Irish suffragettes did not welcome what they felt was interference in their own struggles. Margaret wrote in the *Irish Citizen*, 'the IWFL had no connection with or knowledge of the action of English suffragettes in Dublin ...'[6] For Margaret, the battle was theirs alone but she was soon to step out of the limelight and leave Ireland for good.

Margaret and James emigrated to Liverpool in 1913 after Margaret's time in jail, but they had no intention of stopping their work for the women's movement. After a brief stint in the UK, they moved to India in 1915 where James had been offered work editing Annie Besant's Madras-based newspaper, *New India*. Margaret co-founded the Women's Indian

Association with Dorothy Jinarajadasa and Annie Besant which had over 2,000 members in Madras alone. It aimed to pressure the government into granting the vote to Indian women. She became editor of their journal, the *Stri Dharma* and went on in 1922 to become the first female magistrate in India.

She was jailed again in 1932, for speaking against the Emergency Measures which endeavoured to counteract civil disobedience and deal with the terrorist movement in Bengal, and for supporting Gandhi's free-speech campaign. She spent a year in Vellore Women's Jail and went on to write two books on Indian women's rights amongst other works, as well as becoming the president of the All India Women's Conference in 1938.

Margaret became ill in 1943 after she had a stroke. She was cared for by her husband until her death in 1954 in Adyar, India. Her ashes were spread on the Ganges river.

Kathleen Emerson (later Nicholls) (1885–1970)

Kathleen Maude Emerson was born around 1885 to a Protestant family headed by William and Robina Holmes. William, who was from County Meath, was a stationmaster with the Great Southern and Western Railways and her mother, from County Cavan, was an early member of the IWFL. In 1901, the family were living in Roscrea, County Tipperary. Kathleen married Revd George Emerson in 1910 but while on a trip to Ottawa in Canada in April 1911, Revd Emerson died, leaving Kathleen a widow. By the 1911 census, Kathleen was once again living with her parents, who had moved to the Rathmines and Rathgar area of Dublin, along with brothers Abel and Edward and her sister, Helen.

Kathleen followed her mother into the ranks of the IWFL. In 1911 Kathleen was their secretary, but Kathleen was no bookworm. In the February of 1912, Kathleen travelled to London to join other militant suffragettes as they smashed windows in the city centre. The WSPU organised two days of action in March. On the 1st of the month over 150 women smashed windows in Regent Street, Piccadilly, the Strand, Oxford Street and Bond Street, with stones and hammers. They organised another demonstration on 4 March, aimed at the government offices in Whitehall. Over 200 suffragettes were arrested and jailed for their militant action. Kathleen had been a part of the first wave of violence and was sentenced to two months' hard labour in Holloway Prison.

During her time in Holloway, Kathleen wrote two poems that were published in the WSPU's 'Holloway Jingles' pamphlet:

The Women in Prison

Oh, Holloway, grim Holloway,
With grey, forbidding towers!
Stern are thy walls, but sterner still
Is woman's free, unconquered will.
And though to-day and yesterday
Brought long and lonely hours,
Those spent in captivity
Are stepping-stones to liberty.

Oh! Who Are These in Scant Array

Oh! who are these in scant array
Whom we behold at break of day;
Strange their attire! oh, who are they?
　　The suffragettes in Holloway.

And who are these when chapel's done
Stream out beneath an April sun,
To laugh and jump or shout and run?
    The suffragettes in Holloway.

Who is it say in tones which freeze,
'Pass on this way, convicted, please;
Don't dare to think or breathe or sneeze?'
    The Wardresses in Holloway.

And who is he, tho' grand his air,
Doffs not his hat to ladies fair?
Is it because he has no hair?
    The Governor in Holloway.

Then whilst we eat our frugal food,
Who breaks upon our solitude,
And says 'You're all so beastly rude'?
    Why 'Mother's Own' in Holloway.

And who, with sanctimonious drone,
Tells tales of highly moral tone,
Whilst gazing upwards at the dome?
    The Chaplain, sure, in Holloway.

Hark! Who is this with stealthy tread,
Comes round each day to count his dead,
And scalps his victims, so 'tis said?
    The Doctor, in grim Holloway.

But who is this now comes in view,
His smiling face cheers others too?
Father M'Carroll, 'here's to you,'
    The only Man in Holloway.

> But there is one we'll ne'er forget,
> She says she's not – and yet and yet
> We feel she is a Suffragette?
> > The Matron dear, of Holloway.[1]

Back in Dublin, Kathleen continued her involvement in the suffragette movement. When Prime Minister Asquith visited Dublin, Kathleen was caught up in the anti-suffragette chaos that ensued. As she was walking along Eden Quay, she was thrown to the ground and viciously kicked. There were cries of 'Throw the suffs in the Liffey!' but Kathleen was rescued before it could happen. Unperturbed by the violence, Kathleen was back in action at the Dublin Horse Show where she heckled Lord Aberdeen on the force-feeding of women prisoners before being forcibly removed.

Force-feeding was usually done through the mouth but was sometimes through the nostrils via a tube that led down the throat and into the stomach. Different mixtures of nutrients were used but were typically milk and brandy. The women were held down by a medical officer and the matron or attending staff, and in the case of nasal feeding, a wooden or steel gag was placed in their mouths. A funnel at the end of the tube was filled with the liquid food and poured through the tube into the stomach. Apart from the procedure being horrendous, it could introduce fluid into the lungs causing pleurisy and/or pneumonia.

In November of 1912, Kathleen returned to smashing windows at the Custom House on the Dublin quays, breaking six panes of glass with Margaret Connery. The damage was estimated at £5 and they were apprehended by Constable McQuaid who took them to Store Street police station. Margaret Palmer and Frank Sheehy Skeffington visited them there to offer bail.

In court on the 7 November 1912, Kathleen said that 'breaking windows was too small a protest, nothing short of a bomb would adequately express her feelings'.[2] Both women were given a fine or fourteen days' imprisonment in Mountjoy Jail. They refused to pay their fine on principle. In a letter Kathleen wrote to the chairman of the General Prisons Board, she says, 'For having broken windows in the Custom House in connection with the Suffrage Agitation I have been fined by Mr McInerney the sum of £1 and as to pay a fine is altogether against my principles, I have been sent here sentenced to fourteen days'. She goes on to say, 'In view of the fact that the Board granted certain concessions to four suffrage prisoners, Mrs Sheehy Skeffington, Mrs Palmer and the Misses Murphy who were convicted in June last for a precisely similar offence, I would beg therefore that to me also the same privileges be allowed'.[3] The women were allowed to have their food supplied from outside, to receive books and papers and to receive one visit daily. Kathleen went on hunger strike while she was in prison but she was not forcibly fed.

On Kathleen's prison record, it is noted that she had previously been detained in Holloway Prison as a suffragette and that her former prisoner character had been 'good'. Kathleen and Margaret were both released on 20 November, just two days after they were committed. The *Irish Independent* mentioned in their cover of the release that 'their fines have been paid anonymously'.[4]

In 1913, Kathleen decided to stay in Tullamore, which had been redesignated as the prison to house suffragettes. Kathleen wanted to act as a support for the women and to watch out for any developments that may occur that the rest of the suffragette movement should be informed about. She was later also charged with assaulting a DMP constable which she admitted to but said she did not regret. The charge was later withdrawn.

Emerson resigned as secretary of the IWFL in the summer of 1914 and turned her thoughts to expressing herself through literature. Kathleen wrote poetry and short stories and in 1915, Kathleen was busy writing for the *Irish Citizen*. She had a story published entitled 'The Deserter' which had a strong anti-war message. She also wrote 'Whitening Unto Harvest' which attacked the church and State for legitimising war babies and she went on to write memoirs of Francis Sheehy Skeffington and James Connolly.

In late 1919, Kathleen Emerson married Harry Nicholls and her political life seems to have grown quiet. Her husband was from Derry and he worked as an engineer for the Dublin Corporation but he was also an officer with the Irish Volunteers and had been active during the 1916 rising. Kathleen was in her 80s when she died in 1970, after many years of ill-health. Harry died five years later and is buried with his siblings in St Patrick's Cemetery, Enniskerry, County Wicklow.

Mabel Purser
(1873–1957)

Mabel was born Lucy Mabel O'Brien in Donegal in 1873 to the Very Revd Lucius Henry O'Brien and Emily Mary (*née* Montgomery). She was one of seven children and their second-born daughter. Mabel's father was the Dean of Limerick and she came from an illustrious family. Her grandfather was William Smith O'Brien, leader of the Young Ireland movement, Irish nationalist and MP. He was sentenced to hang for his part in the 1848 rising but was later transported to Van Diemen's Land. Her cousin, Stephen Gwynn, was also an MP.

Mabel married Francis Carmichael Purser, a physician, in Limerick on 9 December 1902. Around the time of the suffragette move to militancy, Mabel was living with her husband at 20 Lower Baggot Street. They had three daughters, Elizabeth, Emily and Honor (named after her older sister) and a son, John. Also living with the household was their cook, parlourmaid and nurse. Mabel moved in high society circles and a newspaper article at the time mentions how shocked her peers were to find out she was involved in the suffrage movement.

Mabel was convicted of wilfully damaging glass on 30 January 1913. She had been smashing windows two nights after Margaret Connery, Margaret Cousins and Barbara Hoskins had been arrested for maliciously damaging glass. At her sentencing, she is reported to have said that she wanted to give the lie to the statement made in the House of Commons that Irish women did not want the vote.

Margaret Connery, Margaret Cousins and Barbara Hoskins were sent to Tullamore Prison on 28 January and Mabel followed them on 5 February, after a short spell in Mountjoy. Her grandfather had also been incarcerated in Tullamore and she must have felt a sense of following in his footsteps as she entered the building. In other times, when she was selling suffrage papers, she stood under his memorial statue in O'Connell Street, Dublin city centre.

All of the women went on hunger strike in their protest against not being given the status of political prisoners and the privileges they should be entitled to. Mabel starved herself for two weeks but was not forcibly fed.

When the two Margarets and Barbara were released, the IWFL held a reception for them. Margaret Cousins informed the meeting that they should 'send a message of good cheer and remembrance' to Mabel who was still serving her time.[1] Mabel was freed on 17 March, having been released early on commutation of sentence.

Mabel's daughter, Dr Elizabeth Fitzpatrick, later told of Mabel's involvement in the fight for the right to vote. These conversations have been recorded as the Harrison tapes and are available at the The Women's Library, London.

Little is known about Mabel's later years. Her husband, Francis, became a professor of neurology at Dublin University. They kept homes at Fitzwilliam Place in Dublin and Knockraheen House, County Wicklow. Francis died suddenly in 1934 and Mabel outlived him by many years, dying in June 195. She is buried in Calary church, County Wicklow, along with her husband and their daughter, Elizabeth.

Hanna Sheehy Skeffington (1877–1946)

Johanna (Hanna) was born in Kanturk, County Cork in 1877. She came from a political background where her father and uncle were activists in the fight for Ireland's freedom. Her father, David Sheehy, was involved in the Irish Republican Brotherhood, being imprisoned six times for revolutionary activities, and was an active member of the Land League.

Her family moved to Drumcondra in 1887 where Hanna studied languages in St Mary's University College for Women. She was the first woman to graduate from the college gaining a BA in modern languages in 1899, and went on to study in Germany and France before returning to achieve first-class honours in her MA in modern languages in 1902. It was during this year that she was approached to sign a petition for women's suffrage and it opened her eyes to the world of women's rights. She said, 'Naturally I signed and became a conscious suffragist from that hour on'.[1]

Hanna married Francis Skeffington in June 1903 and they famously took each other's names as their marital surname at a time when women usually took their husband's name. Francis was politically active and a supporter of the women's suffrage movement as well as women's right to education. In 1904,

Hanna Sheehy Skeffington and Mrs Pearse. (© National Library of Ireland)

he resigned from his job as registrar of the Royal University in protest at their non-recognition of female graduates. Both Hanna and her husband joined the IWSLGA but grew disillusioned by its inability to take militant action which they felt was the only way women would ever achieve the vote.

Hanna founded the IWFL in 1908 in response to what she felt was inactivity on the part of the IWSLGA. She established this new group with Margaret Cousins primarily to push forward the suffrage cause and to instigate more militant methods in trying to obtain the vote. She wrote for several publications, including *Bean na hÉireann* and the *Nation* newspaper, before founding the suffragette newspaper, the *Irish Citizen*, with her husband in 1912. Both Francis and James, Margaret's husband, were to become the editors of the most important means of communication in the Irish suffragette world.

Hanna was soon to act on behalf of women's suffrage. She was convicted of wilfully damaging glass on 20 June 1912 at Dublin Castle along with Jane and Margaret Murphy and Margaret Palmer, and sentenced to a month in jail.

They were imprisoned in Mountjoy where they were allowed the privileges of political prisoners. In the General Prison Board papers, it states, 'they were allowed to talk at exercise and to work together and talk four afternoons a week'.[2]

She became a member of the IWWU at its inception in 1911 and actively helped the workers of the Dublin Lockout in 1913 which occurred after the Dublin tram strike and saw thousands of workers who supported the strike 'locked out' from their workplace. Hanna attended the soup kitchens and handing out of blankets and household essentials with Delia Larkin, Constance de Markievicz and other suffragettes. She was jailed again for assaulting a policeman in November of the same year. Hanna tried to present Bonar Law, the Conservative leader, and Sir Edward Carson, the Ulster Unionist leader, with leaflets but ended up being arrested and sent to Mountjoy. This time she went on hunger strike for five days until her release but was not forcibly fed during this time.

On 13 December 1913, Hanna wrote in the *Irish Citizen*:

> I desire through the medium of the Irish Citizen to thank most heartily all my friends in the Franchise League who worked so strenuously during my imprisonment, and who organised the fine series of protest meetings outside Mountjoy Prison on my behalf. Their splendid enthusiasm and matchless energy were the battering ram that forced open the jail gates! It is gratifying to realise that Sergeant Thomas, by his assault on me, and the police who illegally attempted to break up the protest meetings, have unwittingly rendered us a great service, and given a fine impetus to our movement by rousing public indignation against police methods and the ways of police magistrates. I congratulate the IWFL on its victory over the police, those arch-disturbers of the peace, who were afraid to face even a Police court judgment of their disgraceful conduct. During this period of enforced inactivity I am happy to know that our work goes

forward unimpeded, and that the Franchise League keeps its flag flying, no matter how many of us fall by the way.[3]

Writing for the *Irish Citizen* was one way in which she could always get her message across. When Hanna's father voted against women's suffrage as an Irish Party MP, she publicly denounced him and used the *Irish Citizen* to voice her dismay.

Hanna was actively involved in the Easter Rising in 1916, carrying food and messages to the GPO. It was there that her uncle, Revd Eugene Sheehy, was attending the rebels as their priest and spiritual counsellor. It was to be one of the most terrible times in her life and its consequences drove her to campaign against the British government and align her support to Sinn Fein. Her husband, Francis, was arrested on 25 April, while trying to stop the looting in Dublin city centre and the next day he was taken from his cell and shot without trial with two other prisoners. Hanna did not find what had happened to her husband for days and had to endure British soldiers raiding her home and searching Francis' effects. When she was eventually told, she wanted justice and campaigned for an inquiry into her husband's death that led to his killer, Captain J.C. Bowen-Colthurst, being court-martialled. The British government offered her £10,000 in compensation for Francis' death, which she refused to take.

It pushed Hanna to campaign passionately against British militarism. Hanna left Ireland in December 1916 to tour the US, speaking at over 250 meetings in every state to raise awareness of the situation in Ireland and talk about her involvement in Sinn Fein and the War of Independence. During this time she produced a pamphlet entitled 'British militarism as I have known it' which was banned in the UK and Ireland. On her return to Ireland she was arrested with Maud Gonne-MacBride, Kathleen Clarke and Constance de Markievicz and sent to Holloway Prison in London. Hanna again went on hunger strike until her release.

On her return to Ireland in 1917, Hanna joined the executive of Sinn Fein and resumed her position as editor of the *Irish Citizen* until its closure in 1920. In the same year, she became a councillor for Dublin Corporation, continuing her political career by joining Fianna Fáil in 1926 but only staying on their executive for a year.

Hanna went travelling in 1929 to Vienna and Prague. In Prague, she attended a conference of the Women's International League for Peace and Freedom (WILPF) with Rosamund Jacob. She later became secretary of the Irish Friends of Soviet Russia in support of their revolution and to improve the relationship between Russia and Ireland. This connection saw her attending a conference in Moscow on behalf of the society with Maud Gonne and Charlotte Despard in 1930.

By 1931, Hanna was working as editor of the *Republican File* and later *An Phoblacht*, the journal of the Irish Republican

The Sheehy Skeffinton burial plot. (© J.R. Webb)

Army. Since the *Irish Citizen* had folded, Hanna had written for other newspapers including *Irish World*, *Irish Press* and the *Irish Independent*. She wrote constantly, expressing her views and rallying support for feminism and women's rights over the course of many years.

Her views were to land her in trouble with the authorities yet again, when she was jailed for another month for protesting at a public meeting in Newry to demand the release of republican prisoners. The Northern Irish government had banned her from crossing the border because of her political record. She was detained for ten days before trial and sent to Armagh Jail.

Hanna was still fighting for women's inclusion in politics when she was 66. At this age, she stood for the Dail in the general election of 1943 as an Independent candidate, backed by the Women's Social and Progressive League, the Women Graduates' Association, the Irish Countrywomen's Association, the Irish Housewives' Committee and the Women Citizens' Association. She aimed to fight for equal pay and equal opportunities for women, but her plans were thwarted when she was defeated.

Hanna had spent all her life working for causes, acting with militant fervour when needed and never being afraid to express her views, many of which were written up and printed in various publications. The *Irish Citizen*, which contained many of Hanna's articles and editorials, can be viewed in the National Library of Ireland today along with many of her personal papers and suffrage mementoes.

Hanna died in 1946 and was buried in Glasnevin Cemetery, as was her husband after his remains were removed from Portobello Barracks.

Marguerite Palmer
(1886–?)

Marguerite was born Marguerite Blanche Bannister in 1886 in Newtownards, County Down. She married R.J. Palmer from County Wexford in 1910 and became known as Marguerite or Margaret Palmer (her prison records show several different version of her name). She was one of the suffragettes that boycotted the 1911 census but her husband is listed along with his mother, Eliza, who entered her status as being 'unenfranchised' on their return to 56 Beechwood Avenue in Rathmines. Her husband is listed as a clerk for a wholesale rubber tyre company but he was also concerned with the suffrage movement and supported Marguerite in her work for women's rights, becoming a member of the IWFL, as she did before her marriage.

Marguerite is one of several suffragettes, including Margaret Connery, mentioned the *Aberdeen Journal* of November 1911 for causing an obstruction in the vicinity of Parliament Square, Whitehall and the Strand in London amidst mass demonstrations for the right to vote. For her part in the protests, she was sentenced to a week's imprisonment in Holloway.

Marguerite was one of the foremost members of the IWFL and had joined at its inception, going on to become its honorary secretary. She was a close companion of Hanna Sheehy Skeffington and both of these women held a meeting of the IWFL in the Phoenix Park where over 1,000 women interested in the suffrage movement attended. They shared the platform, addressing the crowd and explaining why they were willing to be imprisoned for their cause.

Marguerite was convicted of wilfully damaging glass along with the Murphy sisters and Hanna Sheehy Skeffington. At their conviction, the court was filled with around 200 women who handed the suffragettes bouquets of flowers as they took the stand on the 20 June 1912. Imprisoned in Mountjoy Jail, they were allowed the privileges of first-class misdemeanants including being able to talk and exercise. However, they went on hunger strike in sympathy with the British suffragettes, Gladys Evans and Mary Leigh, who had attacked Prime Minister Asquith with an axe, to the horror of many in the Irish suffrage movement. These ladies were forcibly fed whilst in an Irish jail but none of the Irish suffragettes suffered similar treatment while in an Irish prison.

Marguerite's photo appeared on the front page of the *Irish Citizen*, along with the Murphy sisters and Hanna, under the banner 'Prisoners for Liberty' on 22 June 1912. Among her achievements, it noted that she heckled Mr Birrell at a Law Students Debating Society meeting, heckled Edward Carson at Rathmines Town Hall, organised census resistance and lobbied Irish members on behalf of the IWFL prior to the second reading of the Conciliation Bill. Marguerite was extremely active in the suffrage movement and her actions were to land her in prison for a third time.

Marguerite was convicted again of wilfully damaging glass in the United Irish League offices on 16 May 1913. She was committed to Mountjoy on the 26th for six weeks' imprisonment in default of paying a fine but was then moved to Tullamore with Dora Ryan and Annie Walsh. In Tullamore Jail they were allowed a room in the prison hospital, bedding, a library book and a special diet.

During their imprisonment they went on hunger strike. Marguerite and Annie's husbands wrote to the Lord Lieutenant, asking whether they were allowed to communicate with their friends and receive letters and a daily visit as per political prisoners. The women informed the governor of the prison that unless these privileges were granted they would refuse food, which they did from 13 June. The IWFL issued a statement on their behalf that was published in the *Irish Independent*, stating that this step had been taken 'owing to the continued refusal of the Irish Executive to grant the prisoners the full rights and status of first-class misdemeanants'.[1]

They were released under the Cat and Mouse Act on 18 June. This act enabled the release of prisoners who had been on hunger strike and their subsequent recall to prison once their health had improved. Their date for recommittal was 2 July but none of the women were returned to prison. On 26 July, Marguerite wrote about her experience in the *Irish Citizen*, in an article entitled 'The Tales of the Tullamore Mice'. The article starts:

> Sentenced to six weeks imprisonment for non-payment of fines and compensation imposed for the breaking of the United Irish League fan-light on May 11th, we were taken to Mountjoy prison, and immediately on arrival applied to the Lord Lieutenant and the Prison Board for 1st Division Treatment. It will be remembered that Mr MacInerney, the magistrate who tried us, was prepared to recommend 1st class treatment on condition that we paid the amount of compensation; this, of course, we refused to do, and were accordingly committed as ordinary prisoners. This initial mistake and want of foresight on the part of the magistrate has since been the cause of not only the ruined health of three women, but the ruined prestige of the Irish Prison Authorities.

Marguerite goes on to explain what it felt like to undertake a hunger strike and underlines her commitment to the suffrage movement, and the commitment of all the women involved in the fight for their right to vote.

> To the Hunger-Striker, one day is the same as another, and each hour as it comes is exactly the same as the last. The day is spent sitting upright on one's chair, looking at nothing, doing nothing, but thinking, thinking always. The blood stagnates at the knees, one creeps over to the bed to seek a change of position and get relief,

but none comes. At last, too weak to sit upright, one is forced to lie down – still no relief; every pulse in the body throbs, throbs incessantly, the heart thumps heavily through the body to the back, no sleep will come, and the hours creep slowly, slowly on.

It is this sickening monotony, the awful silence, the ever present evidence of punishment, the barred windows, and above all, the relentless enemy, waiting, watching, to take any possibly advantage as one's bodily strength gives out inch by inch – these are the things which play such mental havoc with the Hunger-Striker.

This, then, is the real meaning of the Hunger-Strike, and to their everlasting honour and glory be it said, that of all the hundreds and hundreds of women who have engaged in it, weak and strong, old and young, rich and poor, there has never been found one to throw up the fight, even in the face of the horror of forcible feeding. Evidence enough this, surely, that a strong principle exists behind the agitation – a principle that no prison cell persecution can stifle, not even in its latest form, the brutal and futile 'Cat and Mouse Act'. This will be fought as dauntlessly and successfully as was forcible feeding, at the cost, no doubt, of many women's lives, but crushed it shall be, and perhaps by then the authorities will have learned the folly of playing with the deeply rooted convictions of earnest reformers, and recognise the wisdom of falling in line with the spirit of the age, by granting the reform we fight for – political treatment for political prisoners.[2]

Little is known of Marguerite in her later years yet she was such a force to be reckoned with, giving her all to the fight for women's suffrage, risking her health by hunger striking and being imprisoned on several occasions. A true suffragette.

The Murphy Sisters

Margaret (or Maggie) and Jane Murphy were the aliases of Leila and Rosalind Garcias de Cadiz. The sisters were born in Madras, India to Thomas de Cadiz who had been a barrister in Trinidad. One of their ancestors was a duke who was given the isles of Cadiz in payment for his military services, hence their name. When their mother, Margareta (*née* Lawder), died the girls were sent to live in Roscommon with her family, the Gunnings.

When the sisters grew older, they moved to Dublin and in 1910 joined the IWFL as well as the British WSPU. They were in London for the Black Friday protest in November 1910 and took part in many protests and demonstrations. In March 1912, they were imprisoned in Holloway for two months' hard labour for glass breaking and went on hunger strike in protest against the suffragettes in Holloway not being recognised as political prisoners. They were both forcibly fed and released on 15 May.

Back in Ireland, they took part in breaking windows at government buildings on 13 June 1912 and were convicted with Hanna Sheehy Skeffington and Marguerite Palmer on the 20th. On their prison records, they are both noted as being 'a female suffrage agitator'. They declined to give their ages and their conduct is noted as 'fair'. The sisters asked for their own doctor, Kathleen Maguire, Jane's dentist and their solicitor to attend them, which was granted, albeit with comment. The Medical Officer in Mountjoy stated, 'I beg to report that I regard her [Margaret Murphy] as a woman of neurotic temperament who suffers from indigestion, an ailment frequently complained of by women of this type'.[1] This in regards to a woman who had just endured forcible feeding while in Holloway.

During their incarceration, Margaret wrote several letters. In one, addressed to the Lord Lieutenant, she asks to be treated as a political prisoner and explains why they committed their crime:

> Now the offence for which I am imprisoned is a strictly political one, I did not break windows for private spite or personal gain, I broke

them as a protest to the Government who have ignored our just demand. We tried very peaceful & constitutional method such as our resolution forwarded from mass meeting demanding a Government amendment to the Home Rule Bill giving votes to Irishwomen, our demand for a deputation etc. These matters having failed we were forced to do, as men had done to gain the vote, have recourse to militant methods, with this exception that, whereas, men had done grievous bodily injury, we have hurt no one, having broken our windows at a time where the Government offices were not occupied & when there was least likelihood of causing a riot or breach of the peace. Our motives are absolutely pure, as we believe that if women had votes such evils as the 'Sweating System', the White Slave Traffic, etc would not exist, or at least would exist with difficulty. We realise that the degradation and sweating of women is a prolific cause of the overcrowding of our Lunatic Asylums and Consumptive Hospitals also the children of these women swell the ranks of the unemployable, being physically unfit. These questions such as the Nursing Bill, the Education Bill etc are subjects which must be taken up by the New Parliament a& we know that such Bills cannot be a success, without the intelligent co-operation of the women & men of the country. Such there are our motives & I would draw your attention to the fact that the Magistrate who tried us, Mr Swifte, acknowledged that our demand was a just one.[2]

Margaret had also tried to send correspondence to Frank Sheehy Skeffington to be published in the *Irish Citizen* but this was forwarded to the governor for instructions as to whether it should be suppressed. The reply was clear:

His Excellency is advised that while there is nothing per se objectionable in these letters, it would form a serious precedent in future cases if these letters were allowed to be sent to the newspapers. The true meaning of the rules is that letters may be written to friends, but it is another matter to carry on a newspaper correspondence.

Leila Cadiz's suffragette medal. (© Simon and Jill Muggleton)

> His Excellency is advised that in the interest of Prison discipline such letters should not be permitted to issue from the Prison.[3]

They were released on 19 August.

In July of 1913, the women were back in court but this time to defend their right to membership of the IWFL. They had been asked to leave the organisation against claims of disloyalty. The sisters took the IWFL to court to enforce their right to being members, but the case was stopped when the Master of Rolls commented that the defendants 'had no more merit than the plaintiffs, all being engaged in a criminal conspiracy'.[4]

In the following years, the sisters became nurses, tending the wounded from the Easter Rising and the First World War. Jane worked in both the Manchester Military Hospital and the King George V Hospital in Dublin until she was severely disabled by a spinal injury that occurred when she was trying to help an injured soldier. The sisters saw out their later lives in south Dublin, living in Martell's Terrace, Kingstown, now known as Dun Laoghaire. They never married, having both lost fiancées during the war, and remained single in their later lives with just each other for company.

Margaret stood by her sister when, in 1926, she sued Doctor T. Gillman Moorhead for assault whilst being a patient in his care at Monkstown Hospital. Jane accused her doctor of shaking her, striking her and assaulting her, but the case was found in his favour; Jane was said to be neurotic and suffering from hysteria. This echoed unsubstantiated comments made by the Medical Officer when they were imprisoned in 1912.

Jane (or Rosalind Garcias de Cadiz) died in 1955. She is buried in Mount Jerome cemetery with her brother, Captain Frederick Cadiz and his son, Lieutenant Commander Gerald Cadiz. Margaret (Leila Gertrude Garcias de Cadiz) died in 1968 in a nursing home in Donnybrook. A medal awarded to Leila for valour in the suffrage movement with the annotation 'Fed by Force 4/3/12' was sold by Bonham's auction house for over £5,000.

Barbara Hoskins
(1876–?)

Little is known about Barbara Hoskins. Her prison record states she was born in 1876.

She was convicted of wilful damage to glass with Margaret Cousins, Margaret Connery and Mabel Purser on 28 January 1913. She began serving her time in Mountjoy Jail and was then transferred to Tullamore.

Barbara was released on health grounds on 8 February, after five days of hunger striking. A telegram for the attention of the Chief Secretary asked 'if they are to be fed forcibly through the nose, will he give a reference to the legal authority for this practice'.[1] It was not given and the women were not forcibly fed, but Barbara had collapsed.

On her release, the IWFL held a reception where she was presented with a medal for her imprisonment in Tullamore Jail.

Kathleen Houston

Kathleen has the honour of being the last Irish suffragette from the Republic to be convicted on Irish soil although some suffragettes from the North were tried after her in 1914 for militant action in Belfast and Lisburn. Kathleen was one of the most militant in the Irish suffrage movement and was imprisoned in the UK and Ireland on several occasions.

Kathleen was secretary of the Dublin branch of the IWFL and a close companion of Hanna Sheehy Skeffington. She began her involvement in the suffrage movement by attending protests and WSPU meetings in London and in November 1910, she was convicted and sentenced to two months' imprisonment in Holloway after the Black Friday riots. After a WSPU meeting at Caxton Hall where the suffragettes were rallied, they marched on Downing Street; Kathleen would have been with the crowd of women who attacked the police, knocking off their helmets, pushing them over and striking them with their umbrellas and placards as the police used force to stop the women getting to their destination. Kathleen was one of over 150 suffrage agitators along with fellow Irish women Mrs J. Earle and Miss Helen McDermott. In a statement published in the press, the WSPU said, 'If the Premier will not give assurance that women shall be franchised next year, they [would] revert to war'.[1]

In 1911, Kathleen was back in London at Bow Street Police Court, to be sentenced to one month's imprisonment. She appeared with several other suffragettes who were being charged for various offences, including breaking windows and malicious damage.

In June 1912, Kathleen, along with other suffragettes who appear in these pages, went on a window-breaking protest in Dublin. She was committed along with Margaret Hasler, Hilda Webb and Maud Lloyd on 12 July for malicious damage to glass. They all received a heavier sentence than previously convicted suffragettes which was six months' imprisonment, but were accorded first-class misdemeanant status. They were allowed the 'usual privileges of class & daily visits & letters granted by [the] Visiting Committee under Rule 231 ... permission also given by government to associate & converse with one another and with four prisoners'.[2] The other prisoners referred to were Hanna Sheehy Skeffington, the Murphy sisters and Margaret Palmer who had been committed three weeks previous to Kathleen's incarceration. Kathleen was due for release on 12 December but was allowed to return home on 8 November 1912.

At the Daffodil Day celebrations held by the IWFL in 1914, Kathleen acted out the part of Joan of Arc, sitting tied to a stake with wood piled up around her as Constance de Markievicz acted out a drama with her that depicted Joan's accession to martyrdom. Kathleen was a good choice for Joan of Arc as she too had decided to do as much for her cause as she possibly could.

In April 1914, Kathleen broke a window at College Green Post Office in protest of the Cat and Mouse Act. She refused to pay her fine for wilful damage to glass and said that she would hunger strike on arrival in prison. True to her word, she was committed on 1 May and began her hunger strike immediately. She was released on medical grounds on the 5th and had not been forcibly fed.

The outbreak of the First World War put a stop to militant suffragette action in Ireland and women were able to vote for the first time in the general elections held after the war if they were over 30 and had certain property or other qualifications. Kathleen was at the forefront of the fight for Irish women to obtain the vote and must have celebrated their success with other members of the IWFL. Little is known about her childhood, family or later life.

The English Suffragettes

Three English suffragettes were convicted and imprisoned in Ireland in 1912. Their actions caused controversy and dissent as well as sympathy amongst the Irish suffragettes. Many said the women had not been asked to become involved in the Irish struggle for the right to vote and they resented their actions, but on their incarceration and subsequent treatment many Irish suffragettes supported these three women.

The British Prime Minister, Asquith, visited Dublin in July 1912. His visit was the cause of several demonstrations and protests. On a visit to Kingstown (Dun Laoghaire), he was hailed through a megaphone by a group of women who had commandeered a boat and were waving their Votes for Women placards to draw attention.

Unbeknown to any of the Irish suffragettes, Mary Leigh, Lizzie Baker and Gladys Evans, three members of the WSPU, had come over to Dublin from London to join in the protests and more specifically to disrupt Asquith's public speeches. Irish militancy had involved nothing more than stone throwing and broken window panes but the WSPU contained hardened militants who had become adept at violent, direct action tactics.

Mary Leigh
(1885—1978)

Mary Leigh (*née* Brown) was born in Manchester in 1885. In 1906, Mary joined the WSPU and later became the drum major of the WSPU Drum and Fife Band that played at protests and marches. Her militant career began in 1908 when Mary was arrested for throwing stones at No. 10 Downing Street and sent to Holloway Prison. Not long after, Mary was protesting at the House of Commons when she grabbed the bridle of a police horse. She was sentenced to three months' imprisonment. In 1909, Mary took to the roof of a building where Asquith was speaking and, after removing the tiles, threw them down onto the police below. For this, she got two weeks more imprisonment. This was to be her first experience of being force-fed through the nose.

Just out of prison, Mary was caught days later throwing stones at David Lloyd George's car. This time she was sent to Strangeways Prison for one month's hard labour and was force-fed again. In 1911, she was imprisoned for two months for assaulting a policeman. By the time she came to Dublin she had been acting as an WSPU militant for several years.

Lizzie Baker
(1866—1951)

Lizzie Baker was born Sarah Jane (Jennie) Hunt in 1866. Lizzie was her alias and after her marriage she also used the name Jennie Baines.

Lizzie joined the WSPU in 1905 and became a paid organiser for them in 1908. Her job was to organise meetings, arrange the disruption of political meetings, open new branches of the WSPU and arrange mass meetings and rallies for which she was paid £2 a week. Lizzie was imprisoned around fifteen times in England for the suffragette cause, including being sentenced to six weeks' imprisonment in 1908 for 'unlawful assembly'. After her appearance in Dublin, she went on to bomb train carriages parked in a siding and was sent to Holloway Prison where she went on hunger strike. This made her severely ill and on her release she emigrated to Australia with her family and became involved in their fight for women's rights there.

Gladys Evans
(1877–?)

Gladys Evans was born in 1877. She was the daughter of the owner of *Vanity Fair*, a British weekly society magazine. In 1908 she was working for Selfridge's until she began running a WSPU shop. Gladys emigrated to Canada in 1911 where her sister was living but returned to the UK in 1912, just before she visited Dublin. Little is known of her later life except that she moved to the US. Her papers regarding the suffrage movement were donated to the New York Public Library.

While in Dublin, these three women threw a hatchet into Asquith's carriage as it entered Nassau Street. Prime Minister Asquith and John Redmond were travelling together and were both unhurt, but the women's actions sparked public outrage. Not content to just scare the prime minister, they also attempted to set fire to the Theatre Royal, where he was due to speak. They set light to the curtains in one of the boxes and caused an explosion. When their rooms were searched, explosives were found. Although the Irish groups denounced their actions, it created a groundswell of animosity towards the movement and the women involved. Newspaper headings at the time reported 'The Hatchet Outrage' and 'The Virago and the Hatchet'.

They were sent for trial on 19 July for throwing the hatchet but the charges were dropped; neither Redmond nor Asquith appeared as witnesses so the case was unable to proceed.

However, on 6 and 7 August, the women were committed for arson, explosion and conspiracy. Lizzie Baker was given seven months' hard labour while Mary Leigh and Gladys Evans were sentenced to five years' imprisonment – a sentence that caused shockwaves throughout the suffrage movement. The women went on hunger strike from the 14 August and were supported by the Irish suffragettes also in Mountjoy Jail, including Hanna Sheehy Skeffington.

Lizzie Baker was released on health grounds four days later but Gladys Evans and Mary Leigh were forcibly fed from the 20th until their release. Mary was released on 21 September while Gladys was released on 3 October, both into hospital care, and they were not recommitted. They were the only suffragettes to be force-fed on Irish soil and it caused a public outcry.

It has been suggested that Irish suffragettes were not force-fed as it was a barbaric and disturbing practice that would have long-term health consequences for the women involved. It may have been that prison staff also refused to give such treatment, but in the case of the British suffragettes there were no such qualms. Mary Leigh was force-fed for forty-six days and Gladys Evans for fifty-eight days.

An editorial in the *Irish Citizen* commented:

... the offences for which Mrs Leigh and her colleagues were arraigned this week cannot be confused with ordinary crime. They are symptoms of a deep-seated political grievance, of political unrest not to be assuaged otherwise than by the removal of that grievance. They are warnings – serious warnings, one may admit, yet mild in comparison with similar manifestations in the past on the part of men suffering injustice – that in the words of Mr Birrell, 'the time for shuffling and delay is past'. For every woman who is goaded to the point of action such as taken by Mrs Leigh and Miss Evans, there are hundreds suffering under a profound sense of indignation at tyrannical government; there are thousands, less profoundly moved, yet deeply in earnest in the struggle for their rights. These hundreds, these thousands, will not be appeased or cowed by the spectacle of prison sacrifices in voicing the sentiments of all. Rather they will be provoked to emulation, to open defiance of the Government, the law, the state of society which makes it possible for women of the hero-type, such as Mrs Leigh, to be ranked with criminals. Tyranny is here, as always, not only a crime, but a blunder.

English law being mainly an assemblage of heterogeneous judicial decisions, not a rationally ordered code, there is, naturally, no consistency in its workings with regard to political prisoners. The Irish suffragettes now in Mountjoy are treated as political prisoners, because their protest did not sufficiently alarm the authorities; the English suffragettes consigned to the same prison last Wednesday, whose political motive is equally manifest, and was commented on and recognised as honest both by judge and prosecuting counsel, are treated as convicts; – because they succeeded in striking terror into the Government, and the first thoughts of terrified tyranny, gauging by its own cowardice the effect of brutality on others, is to resort to savage repression. Another reason, doubtless, was the expectation that the inflaming of popular passion against the English Suffragettes would enable the latter to be degraded and tortured with impunity – an expectation doomed to disappointment in the revulsion of feeling caused by Judge Madden's ferocious sentences, quite as much as by Mrs Leigh's eloquence, amongst the Irish Suffragists who are most sincerely opposed to militancy.[1]

The Belfast Suffragettes

Among the last suffragettes to be convicted in Ireland were the ladies who undertook direct action in the North between March and August of 1914, when southern suffragettes had all but ceased their militant activities. The action was organised through the WSPU and called the Ulster Campaign. Many suffragettes from the South disagreed with their involvement as did the Londonderry Society who were against supporting a militant policy. This did nothing to stop the use of explosives and arson as the women attempted to burn houses and churches as part of their campaign.

Militancy began in Belfast in 1912 when windows of the GPO in Donegall Square in Belfast were smashed. The suffragettes in Ulster were beginning to rally, holding large meetings in places like the Ulster Hall, the Grand Opera House, Ormeau Park, Carlisle Circus and the Methodist College. The direct action continued in 1913 with telephone boxes having their wires cut and postboxes being set alight. It was decided that places of male authority should be targeted to force them to pay attention. To that end, the grandstand at Newtownards Race Course, the teahouse at Bellevue Zoo and Cavehill Bowling and Tennis Club were on the receiving end of militant attacks. The women also poured acid on the greens at Fortwilliam Golf Club.

By 1914, the women began to step up their militant activity. Some of them set fire to Abbeylands House in Whiteabbey, causing £20,000 in damage. Madge Muir and Dorothy Evans were accused of having explosives for unlawful purposes in relation to several fire attacks and were placed on remand on 8 April and sent for trial on the 22nd and 23rd. At their hearing, Madge Muir, a Scottish suffragette, threw her handbag, book and walking stick at the judge and Dorothy Evans had to be physically restrained by policemen. Both women began their hunger strike as soon as they were placed in remand and were released on health grounds four days later. They took up their hunger strike again at their committal but were not forcibly fed and were released under the Cat and Mouse Act.

All the women who were imprisoned during this time were housed in the 'A' wing of Crumlin Road Gaol in Belfast. Madge Muir was arrested again with Mary Lamour and they were committed on 3 June 1914 for setting fire to a dwelling house. They also went on hunger strike and were released under the Cat and Mouse Act. Whereas the southern suffragettes had used glass-breaking as their way of making a point, the Ulster suffragettes used fire. In the early months of 1914, twelve places of male authority were attacked including Wallace Castle, Ballylesson church in Lisburn and Cavehill Bowling and Tennis Club.

Mabel Small was convicted of wilful damage to glass and given a sentence of two months' imprisonment. She was released under the Cat and Mouse Act after hunger striking for four days and was recommitted.

Dorothy Evans, Mrs Carson, Joan Wickham and Lilian Metge, founder of the Lisburn Suffrage Society and treasurer of the Irish Women's Suffrage Society (IWSS), were sent for trial after attempting to blow up Lisburn Cathedral on 31 July 1914. They were tried on 8 August and began a hunger strike that lasted until their release on the 12th.

Three days later, Joan Wickham and Mrs Carson were sentenced for malicious damage to glass. They were released on the condition that they refrained from committing acts of violence during the national crisis (the First World War). They signed an undertaking that reads 'in view of the present crisis in which our country is involved, we hereby undertake not to commit any further militancy while the policy of the WSPU remains as at present, conditioned on our release and being sent home without abuse'.[1]

The women involved in the Ulster Campaign were both Irish and English. Lilian Metge, leader of the Lisburn Suffrage Society, for example, was descended from a well-to-do Quaker family. Her father, Richard Cambridge Grubb was from Tipperary and her mother was Harriet Richardson, daughter of Jonathon Richardson who was a Lisburn MP in the 1850s. Lilian lived in Seymour Street and married R.H. Metge from County Meath but was widowed before she was 30. As well as founding the Lisburn Suffrage Society, she represented the IWSF in Budapest at the International Suffrage Congress held in 1913.

Dorothy Evans was an English suffragette sent over to the North by the WSPU to help organise their Ulster Campaign. She grew up in South Norwood, London, was educated at the North London Collegiate School and trained as a gymnastics teacher at Dartford College. She became a member of the WSPU in 1907 while at college. Her career as a suffragette began in 1909 when she heckled a cabinet minister and threw stones. During the next five years she was arrested nine times for various militant actions and was imprisoned on several occasions. She used the tactic of hunger striking on her incarcerations and was force-fed a number of times while in prison in the UK. She took over the London offices of the WSPU when the Pankhursts fled to France, fearing imprisonment. On their return, she was sent to Bristol and then to Northern Ireland where she was arrested with Madge Muir.

This spate of violence ended as the First World War gathered pace and the WSPU pulled out of Ulster, leaving it back in the care of the IWFL, the Church League for Women's Suffrage and the Northern Committee of the IWSF. Militant activity stopped well before the vote was achieved but the women had made their point.

The Political Suffragettes

Anna Haslam
(1829–1922)

Anna Haslam was born in 1829 to a Quaker family living in Youghal, County Cork. Born Anna Maria Fisher, she married Thomas Haslam in 1854 who was also from a Quaker family residing in Mountmellick, County Laois and they moved to Dublin in 1858. Anna spent her early life teaching knitting and lacemaking to young girls and she established her own lacemaking business that she then passed on to the Presentation nuns. She attended a talk in Blackrock by Anne Robertson, a feminist speaker, around 1858 and was inspired her to join the suffrage movement and organise further meetings for feminist speakers to spread the message of women's empowerment and advocate for the right to vote.

In 1866, the first petition seeking suffrage for women was presented to the House of Commons by John Stuart Mill. Twenty-five Irish women had added their signatures, including Anna. Mill corresponded with Thomas, Anna's husband, over the possibility of setting up an Irish suffrage society in Dublin but Mill felt that the immediate prospects were not encouraging. Although his comments may have delayed the setting up of such a society, Anna and Thomas were not to be deterred.

In the February of 1876, Anna, along with her husband, founded the first Irish suffrage society in Dublin, the DWSA. Its members were mostly Quakers and by 1896, it only had a membership of forty-three but this gradually rose to 647 by 1911. Anna was to spend many years as its secretary, stepping down in 1913 but remaining its life president. Throughout her years as secretary Anna kept diligent records and minutes of meetings that set out the work of the organisation and all its involvement in various campaigns.

The DWSA was a non-militant organisation that aimed to raise public awareness of the suffrage movement and began by engaging women (and men) in discussion at drawing room meetings. These were mostly conducted in the Haslam's home on the Rathmines Road. The association kept a close eye on political developments at home and in the UK and encouraged women to contact their MPs to bring their attention to bills and amendments that would affect women and to seek their support in lobbying for change. Whenever there was debate regarding women's suffrage in the House of Commons, the society called on Irish MPs, influential people and the press to rally to their cause. Thomas also edited a published journal in 1874, *The Women's Advocate*. It only ran to three issues but outlined the DWSA's actions and policies. It was so popular, however, with the English suffragette Lydia Becker that 5,000 copies were printed for dissemination.

The DWSA began sending delegates to feminist conferences and speeches where they met with other women from Ireland and the UK who were mobilising for the right to vote as well as other campaigns, including educational reform and the right for a married woman to control her own property. Anna and her husband regularly travelled to attend other suffrage meetings, conferences and demonstrations. In October of 1896, Anna travelled to Birmingham to attend a national conference. It was here that the idea of joining forces to build a National Union of Women's Suffrage Societies (NUWSS) was discussed and both the DWSA and its Belfast equivalent became founding members.

In 1898 the Local Government Act became a focus of Anne's attentions; it allowed for county councils and urban and rural district councils to be elected and for women with certain property qualifications to be eligible to sit on these new bodies. It became such an important part of the struggle for women's rights that the DWSA changed its name to the IWSLGA. Women were encouraged to become more and more involved in politics on a local level as well as nationally.

Anna travelled to the UK again in 1903 as part of a delegation to attend the Conference of the National Convention in Defence of the Civil Rights of Women. In Holborn Town Hall, plans were made to hold mass general meetings across the UK and Ireland. Returning home, Anna helped to organise the Dublin meeting at the Mansion House on 14 January 1904.

Many of the women featured in this book began their suffrage involvement through the IWSLGA. Younger women wanted to take more militant action but Anna and Thomas Haslam always remained pacifist in their views and their running of the organisation. In 1908, Hanna Sheehy Skeffington, Margaret Cousins and other interested women were discussing the formation of a more militant society, the IWFL. In Margaret's autobiography, she recalls, 'So a group of us went on November 6 to the dear old leader of the constitutional suffragettes, Mrs Anna Haslam, to inform her that we younger women were ready to start a new women's suffrage society on militant lines. She regretted what she felt to be a duplication of effort.'

The Political Suffragettes

Transcript of dedication to Anna and Thomas Haslam. (© J.R. Webb)

The Haslams' memorial seat at St Stephen's Green. (© J.R. Webb)

She may have seemed like an older woman, set in her pacifist ways to the younger generations of suffragettes, but she had established the suffrage movement in Ireland and begun a process that would result in the culmination of all their hopes. Thomas died in 1917 before the General Election of 1918 where women over 30 were allowed to vote for the first time. Anna, however, after years of suffrage involvement, took the opportunity to cast her vote, something that she had worked for all her life. On that day she was presented with a bouquet of flowers in the suffragette colours and was congratulated by many of the women who had followed in her footsteps.

Anna died in 1922, the same year women in Ireland over 21 could vote for parliament on the same basis as men. On St Stephen's Green, there is a stone seat dedicated to the memory of both Anna and Thomas and their commitment to Ireland's suffrage movement and the achievement of the vote for women.

Louie Bennett
(1870–1956)

Born in 1870, Louie had a middle-class background. She attended boarding school in the UK, Alexandra College in Dublin and went on to study music in Bonn, Germany. How she came to be involved in the suffragette movement is unknown but from the late 1800s suffragette societies were emerging in Ireland in response to changing social and political times.

Louie Bennett was involved in the establishment of three organisations: the IWSF, the Irish Women's Reform League (IWRL) and the IWWU. The year 1911 marked Louie Bennett's emergence into the public arena as she became one of Ireland's foremost suffragettes, a trade unionist and peace advocate.

In 1911, the year when women refused to participate in the census in protest of their lack of a vote, Louie joined with Helen Chenevix to establish the IWSF. This absorbed the IWSLGA and local suffrage groups from around the country. By 1913, fifteen groups had joined the organisation including Derry, Lisburn, Belfast, Galway, Waterford and Birr. Contrary to other suffragette organisations, it was non-party political and non-militant, although Louie stated that she would not condemn any woman acting militantly. She saw the aim of the organisation as one of propaganda and education. By working together and women having the vote, it would be beneficial for the welfare of Ireland.

In 1913, she was one of only three Irish women who attended the International Women's Suffrage Alliance in Budapest. The International Alliance was founded by American suffragettes on the principle that women should have equal rights and equal responsibilities. 1913 was also the year of the Dublin Lockout and Louie became more involved in the plight of women and work. She was involved in a scheme with the lady mayoress to aid striker's families and could be found working in the soup kitchens alongside Countess de Markievicz, Hannah Sheehy Skeffington and Delia Larkin.

The IWRL became an important part of her work for women. It campaigned to provide school meals and advocated the technical education of girls. A committee was set up to watch legislation that affected women and the courts were monitored for cases of injustice to women and younger girls. An investigation into women workers in Dublin factories found that they were paid much less than their male counterparts.

Louie's work effectively linked the labour and suffrage movements. However, Louie was reticent in becoming involved in trade unions because she had reservations about

Connolly's policy of combining nationalist and labour activities, as most Irish Nationalist MPs were opposed to giving women the vote. In 1916, she changed her mind and became more involved in trade union affairs. She took over leadership of the IWWU and became editor of the *Irish Citizen*, the suffrage newspaper. In 1917, she became the organisations secretary and stayed in the position until 1955. The IWWU were instrumental in seeking change in women's working conditions, pay and holiday entitlements.

In January 1918, Louie wrote in the *Irish Citizen*:

> The most notable development of the women's movement in Ireland during the past year has been the sudden growth of trade unionism amongst women workers. A year ago the members of the Irish Women Workers Union numbered only a few hundreds: now they are over 2,000. The Munition workers are strongly organised under the national Federation of Women Workers; tailoresses, shirt-makers and other workers with the needle are enrolling in great numbers in all the big towns in the Society of Tailors and Tailoresses. Women clerks are now amongst the keenest and most active members of the Irish Clerical Union and the National Union of Clerks, although this time last year the women clerks of Dublin were still in doubt whether they were not too nice for anything resembling a Union! The most interesting point in regard to this rapid organisation is the spirit in which the women have come into the movement; this spirit promises to atone for their tardiness in entering. They are keen and progressive; quick in their grasp of the fundamental principles of trade unionism, and loyal in adherence to them. The stand the women in the printing trade made during the recent printers' strike was a surprise to many people – not least, perhaps the employers!
>
> Do the women of other classes realise how significant and how far-reaching in effect this development amongst Irish women workers will prove? Hitherto, these women have spent their idealism and loyalty mainly on nationalism. Now their nationalism

Members of the Irish Women Workers' Union. (© National Library of Ireland)

promises to express itself in a practical direction, and women will find the best means of serving Ireland through the power of the trade union. When they have lifted themselves out of the sweated conditions under which they work at present, we shall begin to feel their influence in broader directions and stimulating the civic reforms which all classes' desire but which only workers themselves will ever effectually achieve.[1]

The IWWU also campaigned against conscription in 1918. This was to be a momentous year as the Representation of People Act granted the vote for women over 30 years of age. The Labour Party, impressed by Louie's work, nominated her as a candidate for the general election of 1918. She was their first female candidate. However, Louie declined the invitation.

Louie's interests varied, including travel, politics and more. She attended the 1919 International Congress of Women in Zurich and in 1920 she went to America to

The memorial seat of Louie Bennett and Helen Chenevix. (© J.R. Webb)

raise support against Britain's use of the Black and Tans in Ireland. She was an executive member of the Irish Trade Union Congress 1927–1931 and 1944–1950. She became their first female president in 1932 and again in 1948.

At the IWWU annual convention in 1935, Louie demanded equal status for all workers and a pay scale to reflect wages based on work and not sex discrimination. At this time single women were being paid the lowest wage, single men the middle income and married men the highest. Of course, married women weren't allowed to work at all.

Ten years later, she was still working for female workers' rights when she supported the 1945 laundry strike in aid of a fortnight's paid holiday; 1,500 laundry workers went on strike for fourteen weeks. They worked in conditions that led to tuberculosis and rheumatism, without a break or holiday, and Louie supported their cause through to its successful conclusion. Housing was also an issue for Louie and she campaigned tirelessly for slum clearance and the development of proper housing for the low paid. As she grew older, she also became interested in the need for nuclear disarmament and the banning of nuclear power.

Louie died in her eighty-seventh year, after a lifetime of working for women, whether it was seeking the vote or looking for reform and making women's work conditions better. She had not married or had children, but devoted her life for the good of others. She campaigned and protested throughout her life and fought for causes that we take for granted nowadays.

Charlotte Despard
(1844–1939)

Charlotte was born in Ripple, Kent to Commander John Tracy William French and Margaret (*née* Eccles). Her father was from Frenchpark, County Roscommon and was a naval officer. At the age of 10, after her father died and her mother was committed to an asylum, Charlotte was sent to live with relations in London.

In 1870, Charlotte married Maximilian Carden Despard, an Anglo-Irish businessman who had made a fortune in the Far East by cofounding the Hongkong and Shanghai Bank. He encouraged her love of writing in their early years of marriage and as they travelled abroad, she wrote ten novels and many poems. She was to continue to write poetry, stories and suffrage propaganda throughout her life. After her husband died in 1890, Charlotte suffered a breakdown and when she emerged it was to begin her political life and fight for women's rights. She became involved in charity and poor relief work in Nine Elms, an Irish populated slum district of London and was elected to be a Poor Law Guardian for Lambeth. Her work in Nine Elms included setting up working men's clubs, youth clubs, a health clinic and a soup kitchen. It was at this time that she converted to Catholicism.

Charlotte's life was a tale of two countries; she would be involved in politics and the suffrage movement on both sides of the water. She was a quirky figure, instantly recognised by her peers for wearing leather sandals rather than boots, and a black chiffon mantilla instead of a hat. In 1906, she joined the NUWSS but later joined the WSPU when she felt the NUWSS was not doing enough to secure women's right to vote. Her belief in more militant action to bring about women's suffrage would see her imprisoned in Holloway twice in 1907. Unhappy about the way in which the WSPU was run, she formed another group, the Women's Freedom League, with Teresa Billington-Greig and Edith How-Martyn. This organisation aimed to use moral and constitutional tactics to bring about women's suffrage rather than violent militant acts. Their most famous strategy was of chaining themselves to railings, especially at the Ladies' Gallery in the House of Commons. Part of their work was to address public meetings and Charlotte often travelled to Ireland to talk on their behalf. She worked under the slogan of 'No Taxation without Representation'.

In 1908, she helped Hanna Sheehy Skeffington and Margaret Cousins to set up the IWFL. She was in Ireland to encourage suffragettes not to tell of their whereabouts for the 1911 census and was back in 1913 to aid the lockout workers in Dublin and set up the Irish Worker's College. During 1912, the *Irish Citizen* set up the Despard Fund to raise money so that Charlotte could travel to Ireland regularly and attend many open-air meetings. Charlotte toured the North, speaking in Belfast, Bangor, Coleraine and Londonderry and then back to Dublin, but the Irish suffragettes were wary of the Women's Freedom League becoming involved in their struggle and after action by British suffragettes on Irish soil, the women involved in the Irish movement withdrew their support.

Charlotte ran for election in the 1918 General Election in Battersea as a Labour Party candidate. At the same time, her brother, John French, was the Lord Lieutenant of Ireland who made it his goal to stop the Irish rebels. This was in direct contrast to Charlotte, who was vociferously supporting them. In 1920, Charlotte became involved in Sinn Fein and took a tour of Ireland with Maud Gonne on behalf of the Labour Party Commission of Inquiry. Their job was to report on and collect evidence of atrocities committed by the police and army forces, particularly in Kerry and Cork.

She returned to Ireland for good in 1921. First living in Dublin at Roebuck House, Clonskeagh, County Dublin, with Maud Gonne and later moving to Whitehead, near Belfast in 1933. Maud was a close companion and when she was sentenced to a term in Kilmainham Jail, Charlotte waited outside for twenty days and nights until her release. Although Charlotte was never imprisoned in Ireland, she was seen as a dangerous subversive under the 1927 Public Safety Act and her actions and travel were closely monitored.

She had formed the Women's Prisoners' Defence League with Maud Gonne to offer support and financial aid to Republican prisoners, but in 1923 it was deemed illegal by the Free State government and all of its open meetings were attended and broken up by the police. Charlotte also saw her home regularly raided and was treated with suspicion by the authorities. She was a member of Cumann na mBan during the War of Independence and opposed the Anglo-Irish Treaty. Back in England, she supported the Irish Self

Determination League which had over 20,000 members, all of whom were of Irish birth or descent. Its members were persecuted by the British government who deported many of them back to Ireland.

In 1930, Charlotte was with Hanna Sheehy Skeffington when she visited Russia and, like Hanna, became a member of the Friends of Soviet Russia organisation. It also prompted Charlotte to join the Communist Party.

In 1937, Charlotte attended her ninety-third birthday party organised by the Women's Freedom League in London. Two years later she was to die in a fall at her home in Belfast. She was returned to Ireland to be buried in Glasnevin Cemetery, close to her friend Constance de Markievicz. Her name lives on in a street named after her in Battersea, Charlotte Despard Avenue, and in Archway there is a pub, The Charlotte Despard, named in her honour.

Maud Gonne
(1866–1953)

Maud was born in Tongham, near Aldershot, Surrey in December 1866, to Captain Thomas Gonne of the 17th Lancers and Edith Frith (*née* Cook). After her mother died in 1871, Maud was sent to a boarding school in France. In 1882, Maud's father was posted to the Curragh and she went with him to settle into life in Kildare but it wasn't long before Maud was involved in women's rights, particularly the work of the Women's Land League. She spent some time in Donegal, working on their behalf to help those who had been evicted, earning herself the name 'The Woman of the Sidhe'.

Whilst Maud was in France she fell in love with Lucien Millevoye, a right-wing politician and journalist who supported the return of Alsace-Lorraine to France.

He inspired Maud's political inclinations and both of them began to work for Irish independence and the release of political prisoners.

In 1889, she met W.B. Yeats who fell in love with her, but Maud returned to France and began an affair with Lucien, having two children by him, Georges and Iseult. In 1902, Maud starred in Yeats' play, *Cathleen Ni Houlihan*, that symbolised Ireland's struggle against British rule. She inspired much of Yeats' poetry but continually refused to marry him and instead married John MacBride in 1903. The marriage would end unhappily with Maud staying in Paris to raise their son, Sean MacBride, whilst John returned to Ireland.

Much has been made of Maud's love life but her real passion was the fight against women's exclusion from political life. Maud was a feminist and a strong believer in women's rights. She founded Inghinidhe na hÉireann (Daughters of Ireland) in 1900. The organisation was set up to allow women who were excluded from nationalist organisations to meet and work towards political change. It had nationalism at its heart and although many of the women involved were suffrage supporters, they wanted rights in an independent Ireland. One of their first acts was to hold the Patriotic Children's Treat in Phoenix Park for over 30,000 children in protest against Queen Victoria's visit to Ireland and the Children's Treat that was held in her honour.

Inghinidhe na hÉireann were represented at the mass meeting of suffragettes and suffrage societies in June 1912 and Maud sent a message of support to its organisers. Although Maud supported the suffrage movement, she disagreed with the IWFL for what she saw as co-operation with British suffragist organisations. Maud was a staunch nationalist and refused to have the vote for women if it meant the vote was used to elect a British government; although Maud was not a militant suffragette, nor wished to be involved in suffrage societies that worked alongside British societies, she firmly believed in a woman's right to vote in a free and just Ireland. It wasn't all discord, however. Maud worked with Hanna Sheehy Skeffington on several

Maud Gonne. (© National Library of Ireland)

issues, one of which being the need to feed school children healthy meals. When told that to authorise their meals it would take a special Act of Parliament, Hanna wrote the act and Maud took it to London. When it wasn't approved, the IWFL with Inghinidhe na hÉireann and trade union support formed their own feeding committee to provide meals to school children in need.

In 1914, Inghinidhe na hÉireann merged into Cumann na mBan, the female section of the Irish Volunteers. Many of the women who were part of this new society were active in the Easter Rising but Maud was in France and absent when her husband was executed. In 1917, Maud returned to Ireland, wearing mourning black, and began to use her husband's name again.

In 1918, Maud was imprisoned in Holloway as a political agitator along with Constance de Markievicz and Kathleen Clarke. They were accused of being involved in the 'German Plot' – a plot to support Germany's takeover of Britain. Maud spoke about her experience in Holloway at an IWFL meeting which was subsequently published in the *Irish Citizen* in 1919. In it she describes the prison, saying:

> I believe there is lodging for some 3,000 prisoners, and it seems always crowded. There are four stories of cells in most of the wings which ray out star fish fashion from a central building between them, are narrow, black, asphalted yards where in dreary rings the prisoners take their exercise; no sun penetrates in some of these, the surrounding buildings are too high; no flowers or creepers here, only black coal or coke dumps. I was told by the wardress that there was a large exercise ground with grass in the middle in another part of the prison, but I never saw it. Mrs Clarke, Countess Markievicz, and myself exercised in a small asphalted yard with a coke dump on one side as high as the second storey, when the wind blew the fine dust from it used to hurt our eyes, and in conjunction with

the ill-ventilated cells was, I think, the cause of the lung trouble I developed …

After we were transferred to hospital we used to exercise in the hospital yard on an asphalt path surrounding a grass patch and a geranium bed. On the grass the bandages used in the hospital used to be dried, and sometimes mattresses aired after disinfection. There was a hedge of Michaelmas daisies, there was also a never-ending procession of poor syphilitic women going into the hospital surgery for treatment …

The air in the cells was so bad that no growing flower could survive more than three days without its leaves withering and turning yellow. Our friends often sent us plants, but not even the hardiest geranium would survive till we discovered that by leaving them in the exercise yard alternate nights we were able to prolong their lives, and we generally descended to the exercise ground each carrying her pot of flowers.[1]

Maud Gonne's final resting place. (© J.R. Webb)

She was imprisoned again in 1923 along with ninety other suffragettes in Kilmainham Jail for protesting at a rally and was released after going on hunger strike for twenty days when her health started to suffer. Charlotte Despard had been waiting for her all that time, keeping her vigil outside the gates. Maud and Hanna Sheehy Skeffington would also have a lasting relationship although they didn't always agree with each other's views. In 1930, they were both members of the Irish branch of the Friends of Soviet Russia and attended their Moscow conference together. They were also involved in the Women's Republican Prisoners' Defence League and Maud presented Hanna with a medal for the work she had done on their behalf.

Maud published her autobiography, *A Servant of the Queen*, in 1938. The 'queen' referred to Cathleen ni Houlihan rather than any British queen, who Maud romantically thought she had seen. In it, Maude recounts her early years but glosses over anything scandalous, such as her relationship with Lucien Millevoye, whether she had a physical relationship with Yeats and what the true nature of their friendship was. In her book, she instead concentrates on her political interests, her patriotism and her activism up until her marriage to John MacBride in 1903. Maud is still recognised for this today.

Maud died in 1953 at the age of 86, in Roebuck House, Clonskeagh (formerly Charlotte Despard's home) and is buried in the Republican plot at Glasnevin cemetery.

Eva Gore-Booth
(1870–1926)

Eva Gore-Booth was born at Lissadell House, County Sligo in 1870. She was the younger sister of the infamous Constance de Markievicz and spent her early years growing up in the environs of a landed estate. Although Eva did not follow her sister into the fight for Ireland's independence, she was committed to the suffrage movement throughout her life in Ireland and Britain.

Eva became ill in 1895 and as a result left Ireland to convalesce in Bordighera, Italy. It was here that she met Esther Roper, her lifelong lover and companion. Esther was several years older than Eva and had been one of the first women to graduate from Victoria University in Manchester. She had been working for some time on the campaign for women's suffrage in the city and her beliefs must have rubbed off on Eva.

In 1896, Eva was back at home and helping Constance to form the Sligo Women's Suffrage Association. Eva became its secretary while Constance was its president, but it wasn't long before Eva left Ireland to live in Manchester with Esther. There they both became involved in the women's trade union movement as well as the fight for suffrage. Eva joined the Manchester, Salford and District Women's Trade Union Council in 1900 and soon became one of its secretaries. She gave talks to meetings of the Independent Labour Party and the Women's Co-operative Guild, beginning a long career of public speaking on the issues she felt strongly about, including addressing a mass meeting of textile workers in Wigan.

Eva spent months in 1900 and 1901 collecting the signatures of female textile workers from Lancashire asking for women's suffrage. In March 1901, the petition, with over 30,000 signatories, was presented to parliament. This was followed by another petition signed by women from the Yorkshire and Cheshire regions. Eva didn't stop there. In 1902, both Eva and Esther collected signatures for a petition calling for women's right to vote. This time it was signed by female graduates all over the UK and Ireland, one of whom was Hanna Sheehy Skeffington. During this year, Eva also set up a new union with Sarah Dickenson, the Salford

Eva and Constance Gore-Booth. (© National Library of Ireland)

and District Association of Power Loom Weavers. She went on to help form the Lancashire and Cheshire Women Textile and Other Workers Representation Committee a year later, with a view to supporting a female candidate who would fight for suffrage in the general election.

Eva mentored Christabel Pankhurst for three years as they worked together for women's right to vote through the North of England Society for Women's Suffrage (NESWS). Christabel was a regular visitor to the couple's home in Victoria Park and was especially close to Eva. Eva supported the establishment of the WSPU in 1903, formed by Christabel with her mother, Emmeline, and two sisters, Adele and Sylvia. But Eva, unlike her sister, was a pacifist at heart and disassociated herself with the group when more militant suffragette action began taking place.

When there was dissent over Christabel's interruption of a meeting at the Free Trade Hall in 1905 where Sir Edward Grey was speaking, Esther and Eva left the NESWS. But they were still firmly committed to the women's movement. In 1906, Eva and other prominent suffragists met with the new Liberal Prime Minister Campbell-Bannerman to demand suffrage, accompanied by fifty Lancastrian female workers. Eva wanted women's suffrage but she also wanted the working women of the North to be included in the right to vote. This was slightly unusual for the suffragette movement, as most of its supporters aimed their efforts at the middle classes. Eva made sure that the concerns of the working class were heard.

In 1907, Eva travelled to various speaking engagements around the country, including a trip to Reading, Berkshire where she gave a talk at the inaugural meeting of a new suffrage society. In 1908, she campaigned against Winston Churchill in the Manchester North-West election which Constance attended and was supported by Adele Pankhurst. When Eva visited Ireland, she spoke to meetings of the IWFL, linking the plight of female mill workers to their lack of the right to vote. Eva continued to raise awareness of the issues facing working women in the north of England and brought their plight to the attention of the suffragists in Ireland.

Eva and Esther also formed the Industrial and Professional Women's Suffrage Society. This society helped to fund the

Rossendale Suffrage Election Committee in order to put forward a suffrage candidate for the general election in 1910, but they were defeated when their candidate, a Liverpool merchant named Arthur Bulley, received very few votes.

In 1913, Eva moved to London with Esther shortly before the outbreak of the First World War. In 1914, they joined the No-Conscription Fellowship that shared their pacifist views. At this point, they resigned membership of the NUWSS as they disagreed with their drive to support the war effort and encourage men to fight in the upcoming conflict. This led them to establish the Women's Peace Crusade with other suffragettes who wanted the government to negotiate for peace.

Eva stayed in London for the rest of her life but was well aware of her sister's involvement in the Easter Rising of 1916. When Constance was given the death sentence for the part she played in fighting against the British, Eva rallied support and successfully campaigned for her sentence to be overturned. She went on to visit her in Holloway Prison in the autumn of 1918, always writing and sending gifts when she couldn't be with her.

As well as campaigning relentlessly for women's suffrage, Eva was also a poet and writer who wrote about women's issues. She co-edited the *Women's Labour News*, a journal for women workers, as well as writing articles and sending correspondence. Eva had been writing poetry for some years; her volume of poetry, *Unseen Kings*, was published in 1904 and *The Death of Fionavar* was published in 1916, amongst other collections and plays. In 1916, Eva and Esther published the journal *Urania* which discussed notions of gender and sexuality and after her death, Esther produced a complete collection of Eva's poems.

Eva died in 1926 of cancer, with Esther at her bedside. Constance did not attend her funeral, claiming she could not face it. Eva was buried in St John's churchyard, Hampstead. Esther had a memorial window created for her in the Round House, Ancoats, which has since been demolished. Eva's lifelong lover and companion survived her by twelve years but was buried with her on her death in 1938.

Mary Hayden
(1862–1942)

Mary was born in Dublin in 1862, the daughter of Dr Thomas Hayden and Mary Anne (*née* Ryan) of Harcourt Street. Her father, Thomas, from County Tipperary was a doctor and a professor in the Catholic University School of Medicine. Little is known of her childhood, but in 1901 she is recorded on the census as living as a boarder in Stamer Street at a house owned by Annie Taylor. She was educated at the Dominican College, Eccles Street and Alexandra College in Dublin. It was here that she first heard debates about women's suffrage which led her to a life of involvement in the fight for women's rights.

Mary achieved a BA in 1885 and an MA in modern languages in 1887 from the Royal University of Ireland. By 1901, she was working as a teacher of English and modern languages. Mary would travel to Greece, India and America over the years, fuelling her love of languages and her interest in modern Greek, Hindustani and Sanskrit amongst others.

From 1909 to 1924, Mary was the first woman to serve on the senate of the National University of Ireland. In 1911, she had moved to the Rathmines Road and was sharing a home with her brother, John, who was a barrister. Mary Hayden was made the first female professor of Modern Irish History in University College, Dublin in the same year, a position she kept until her retirement in 1938. During this time, she actively campaigned for women's rights in the university with her companion, Agnes O'Farrelly. Agnes herself was to become a professor of Irish and is attributed with being the first Irish-language novelist. She was also politically active and a founder member of Cumann na mBan. Her political views must have added to debates between herself and Mary.

The mass meeting of suffrage protesters held in Dublin in June of 1912 was chaired by Mary as a member of the IWSLGA. She oversaw the proceedings and invited each speaker to the platform. She was a long-serving member of the association and became one of their foremost public speakers. She would also speak at meetings of the IWFL, although a pacifist at heart; she disagreed with their more militant methods, and did not undertake any direct militant action.

In 1913, Mary spoke again at a large meeting at the Mansion House in protest against the Cat and Mouse Act. She was joined by Louie Bennett, Dr Kathleen Lynn and Constance de Markievicz – all key women in the suffrage movement. She became president of the National University Women Graduates' Association that year and remained in that position until 1942. In 1915, Mary founded the Irish Catholic Women's Suffrage Association with Mrs Stephen Gwynn, wife of the nationalist MP. This association came later than most of the other suffrage societies but was deemed necessary to specifically include Catholic women in the movement. At its first general meeting in 1916, Mary was thanked for her involvement over the past year when she regularly attended their monthly meetings to give talks on women's issues. Mary was also involved in other organisations like the IWRL and the Gaelic League.

When the vote was partly achieved in 1918, Mary attended the victory celebrations and followed in the procession behind the car that carried the now-elderly Anna Haslam to the William Street Courthouse to vote. It was a day of great celebration that united women across the suffrage movement, regardless of their political inclinations.

As well as being adept at public speaking, Mary was also a competent writer. She wrote many articles and papers on language, literature, history and women's issues. She was published in the *New Ireland Review*, *Freeman's Journal* and the *Irish Citizen* amongst others. She also co-wrote a popular textbook with George Moonan called *A Short History of the Irish People* that was used in schools throughout Ireland for over forty years.

Many women worked for equality way after the right to vote was given. Mary was one of the women involved in contesting the Conditions of Employment Bill in 1935 along with Louie Bennett, Hanna Sheehy Skeffington and Dorothy McArdle. As well as her involvement in debating political issues, she also ran a children's club in her later years. The club, whose patron saint was Joan of Arc, brought out her motherly nature and gave her great pleasure until her death in 1942.

Rosamund Jacob
(1888–1960)

Rosamund was born in Waterford in 1888 to Louis and Henrietta. Her parents were agnostics and firm nationalists, which set them apart from their peers and family. Rosamund attended the local school in Newtown but was unhappy there, perhaps being teased for her parents' beliefs. She was then taught at home by a governess and led a quiet and sometimes lonely childhood, as she mentions in her diaries.

Her interest in politics started in 1906, when Rosamund and her brother, Tom, became founder members of the Sinn Fein Club in Waterford. By 1911, she was actively collecting signatures of Irish Marys for Inghinidhe na hÉireann in response to a collection of signatures that had been presented to Queen Mary of England. Rosamund would always remain a nationalist at heart and would often have to defend her position to suffragettes who felt that women's suffrage was the one and only true cause.

Rosamund lived in her family home in Waterford until her mother's death in 1919. Rather than living a sheltered life, her family entertained many of the leading suffragettes and nationalists: Dr Kathleen Lynn, Hanna Sheehy Skeffington, Helena Moloney, Madeleine ffrench-Mullen and de Valera to name a few. Her childhood may have been lonely but her social circle as she grew older contained some of the country's leading thinkers and activists.

Rosamund had a great interest in politics and the fight for women's rights, but she never took the militant stance that her close friends did. She was involved at an organisational level with the Gaelic League, Sinn Fein, the IWFL, Cumann na mBan, the WILPF, the Irish Women Citizen's and Local Government Association, the Friends of the Soviet Union, the Women's Social and Progressive League and, in later years, the Campaign for Nuclear Disarmament.

When Rosamund travelled to Dublin after her mother's death, she often stayed with Hanna Sheehy Skeffington and they became firm friends. They both shared a love of writing, were nationalists and firm supporters of the women's movement and it was a friendship that was to last their lifetime. When Hanna went to America, Rosamund stayed in her house to take care of Hanna's son, Owen. It was here that she was arrested when the house was raided and Republican propaganda was found. Rosamund was imprisoned in Mountjoy with Dorothy Macardle for four weeks. They also became friends and shared a flat in Rathmines in the coming years.

Rosamund enjoyed writing and wrote several books that showed her interest in politics and feminism. *Callaghan, The Rise of the United Irishmen 1791–1794, The Troubled House, The Rebel's Wife* and *The Raven's Glen* were all published during her lifetime. One of her books, *Third Person Singular*, was published posthumously in 2010 and *Matilda Tone: A Memoir* remains unpublished. Rosamund also wrote short stories and sent correspondence to the *Irish Citizen*, often in reaction to other suffragettes and defending her position as a nationalist.

At a recruiting rally in Wexford in 1914, Rosamund was removed from the platform for displaying a suffragist poster opposing the war. She disagreed with John Redmond's campaign to recruit Irish men to fight for Britain. By 1918, she was canvassing for de Valera to win a seat in the general election but she became disillusioned with politics and resigned from Sinn Fein in 1926, not long after de Valera himself. In 1929, she accompanied Hanna Sheehy Skeffington to Prague to attend the WILPF conference. Although she had been unhappy about political events, she still remained a feminist at heart. Women now had the vote but Rosamund was concerned with their participation in the new Free State and became an active member of the Irish Women Citizen's and Local Government Association to monitor any legislation that would have an impact on women's lives. She also became interested in the political situation in India and travelled to England with Lucy Kingston to hear about Gandhi's methods of non-violent demonstration. After the trip, she joined the committee of the Indian-Irish Independence League and continued her interest in the global position of the women's movement. In 1931, she travelled with Margaret Connery to Russia on behalf of the Friends of the Soviet Union and lectured on her experiences on her return home.

Rosamund spent her life fighting for the causes she believed in. She never married but was the lover of Frank Ryan, a prominent member of the Irish Republican Army, editor of *An Phoblacht* and leader of the Irish Volunteers in the Spanish Civil War. Their relationship was not a public one and Frank had many other relationships, but Rosamund cared for him deeply and wrote about their meetings in her diaries. Perhaps he did not want to commit to their relationship and it is thought to have been over by the 1930s. Rosamund was never linked with any other man.

Rosamund died in October 1960 at the age of 71 after she sustained injuries when she was run over by a car. She never regained consciousness and was buried in the family plot of her friend, Lucy Kingston, in Blackrock. Her papers can be found in the National Library where there is a vast collection of her political and literary papers, as well as 171 diaries that she kept throughout her life that give a close and intimate look at this remarkable woman.

Delia Larkin
(1878–1949)

Delia Larkin was born in 1878 at No. 2 Court, Fermie Street in the Toxeth Park area of Liverpool, to James Larkin and Mary Ann (*née* McNulty). Delia's father died when she was 9 and her older brothers, James and Hugh, became responsible for supporting their widowed mother. Delia also began work at an early age and would forever be linked to her older brother, James (Jim). By the time of the 1911 census, Delia was living with him near Broadstone in Dublin and giving her occupation as a teacher. By this time her brother was extremely influential in the labour movement and had formed the Irish Transport and General Workers Union (ITGWU) with James Connolly.

In 1911, Delia became a founder member of the IWWU, a union that advocated women's rights under the banner of the ITGWU. She advertised the work of the union with a column in the *Irish Worker* where she discussed votes for women, social inequalities and the poor housing conditions of workers. The emphasis on women's suffrage was evident. At the inaugural meeting of the new union it was said that 'a union such as has now been founded will not alone help you to obtain better wages, but will also be a great means of helping you get the vote'.[1] By 1912, the union had 1,000 members, many of whom were also involved in the suffrage movement. In this year, Delia represented the union at several suffrage meetings including Anna Haslam's celebration of the election of Sarah Harrison, Dublin's first female councillor. She attended the mass rally of Irish women to demand that women's suffrage was added to the Home Rule Bill, being held in response to a previous convention to discuss the bill but excluding women. The meeting Delia now attended saw women from all over Ireland attend to discuss their need for suffrage, including women from trade unions and nationalist organisations as well as suffrage societies. She also represented women's interests on Ireland's first trade board where she strived to see poorly paid women working in the manufacturing industry have regulated pay.

Although women's rights were important to Delia, her work was not only about securing the vote for women. The Dublin Lockout saw thousands of workers 'locked out', including 310 women from the Jacob's factory who had gone to work with their IWWU badges on display. Paterson's match factory also locked out its female workers. Delia helped to organise a soup kitchen in Liberty Hall to feed the workers and their families as well as distributing essentials like clothing and blankets. Over

3,000 children received a daily breakfast through the efforts of activist women like Delia, Hanna Sheehy Skeffington and Constance de Markievicz. Suffragettes worked with union members until the lockout ended in 1914 and a bond between the suffrage movement and the labour movement was formed.

The year 1914 also saw a meeting of suffragettes with Augustine Birrell, the Chief Secretary for Ireland, to discuss membership of the newly founded Ladies Advisory Committee. Delia was put forward but rejected, which was seen as a deliberate snub not only to Delia but to the union she had founded. Birrell was never an advocate for women's rights and had previously been attacked by a group of suffragettes in 1910. He disapproved of militancy and suffragettes turning to direct action to emphasis their cause. Why Delia was not chosen is not clear, but she continued her work for women's rights regardless.

Memorial to James and Delia Larkin. (© J.R. Webb)

Delia is also known for organising a union choir to sing at a St Patrick's Night celebration. She went on to form a drama section of the union, the Irish Workers' Dramatic Class, that put on a series of one-act plays on St Stephen's Day in 1912 and Anna fully participated in their delivery. The dramatic class wasn't just a way of entertaining union members; it also raised funds for the IWWU by touring the UK and spread their message to a wider audience.

In 1915, Delia returned to England. Her brother, James, had gone to America leaving the ITGWU in James Connolly's hands. Delia is thought to have worked as a nurse during her time away from Ireland but she returned in 1918 to support the anti-war campaign her brothers were involved in. Things had changed during her absence, however, and a reorganised IWWU refused her membership. This must have been a blow to Delia who had formed the union and been such an integral part of its organisation. In 1920, James Larkin was jailed for criminal anarchy and sent to Sing Sing Prison in New York, sentenced to 5-10 years. Delia contemplated moving to Australia but stayed to support the Release James Larkin campaign and eventually to marry, at the age of 43, Patrick Colgan, a member of the Citizen Army. The campaign was ultimately successful and in 1923 James Larkin was pardoned and returned to Ireland.

Delia remained interested in the labour movement for the rest of her life and joined the Workers' Union of Ireland, where she was involved in another drama group and wrote for the *Irish Worker*. When James became ill, she accepted him into her home in Wellington Road, Ballsbridge and cared for him until his death in 1947.

Delia died in October 1949 and is buried in Glasnevin Cemetery. In 2013, the IWWU Commemorative Committee unveiled a plaque in honour of the IWWU and the women who worked towards change, including Delia Larkin.

Countess Constance de Markievicz (1868–1927)

Constance was born Constance Georgina Gore-Booth at Buckingham Gate, London in 1868. Constance came from an Anglo-Irish background and her father, Sir Henry Gore-Booth, was a baronet and an Arctic explorer who held a landed estate at Lissadell, County Sligo. During the famine, Sir Henry and his wife, Georgina, provided their tenants with free food. Constance grew up in Lissadell House and had a privileged upbringing, although her family's finances were not enough to provide her with an upper-class income. When her father died in 1900, she began to receive £100 a year, which was small in comparison to some of the landed gentry's daughters.

In her early years, Constance wanted to be an artist and studied at the Slade School of Art in London around 1892. Her life in London society brought her closer to the women's movement and the universal appeal for suffrage. While here, she joined the NUWSS. Her sister, Eva, was a strong advocate for women's rights and Constance joined with her to establish the Sligo Women's Suffrage Association of which she was president. In 1896, their first meeting convened in her home at Lissadell House, Drumcliffe, County Sligo.

Constance went on to study at the Académie Julian in Paris. It was here that she met Count Casimir Dunin de Markievicz, a Polish aristocrat who was an artist, playwright and theatre director, whom she would marry in the September of 1900. The marriage made her a countess, mother to a stepson, Stanislaus, and they had a daughter, Maeve, who was raised by Constance's parents. The young couple settled down to married life in Rathmines, Dublin in 1903, where Constance was involved in literary, theatre and the arts circles. In 1905, the countess founded the United Artists Club, which was open to men and women

The Constance Markievicz memorial at Stephen's Green. (© J.R. Webb)

interested in the arts, music and literature, as a place for lively discussion and debate. The club is still in existence and includes many of Ireland's great artists and writers in its membership.

In 1906, Constance rented out a small cottage in the countryside near Dublin that had previously been used by the poet, Pádraic Colum. It is suggested that the copies of *The Peasant* and *Sinn Fein* that he left behind prompted Constance to become involved in the politics of a free

Close-up of Constance Markievicz memorial. (© J.R. Webb)

Ireland. Constance's political life has been well documented in several books including *Renegades: Irish Republican Women 1900–1922* by Ann Matthews, *The Rebel Countess: The Life and Times of Constance Markievicz* by Anne Marreco and *Constance Markievicz: The People's Countess* by Joe McGowan, amongst others.

She was active in Sinn Fein and Inghinidhe na hÉireann. In 1909, Constance was instrumental in founding an organisation to train teenagers to use firearms, known as Fianna Éireann. In 1911, Constance was jailed for disruption after attending an Irish Republican Brotherhood demonstration against the impending visit of King George V. Her political career was underway and she was determined to fight for the causes she believed in.

Although the suffrage movement was to take a back seat as her political inclinations grew stronger, she was still involved in aiding and supporting the movement. On a visit to her sister who was living in Manchester with her companion, Esther Roper, Constance helped the suffrage campaign try to stop Winston Churchill being elected as Manchester North-West's MP. She drove an old-fashioned carriage pulled by four white horses, picked to alert people to the suffrage cause. Flamboyant and eccentric, Constance would prove her point in any way she felt would make a mark.

Constance was at the mass meeting in June 1912, where delegates from many of the suffrage societies demanded women's suffrage was included in the Home Rule Bill. She attended the meeting at Beresford Place that turned sour, and was one of the women who were attacked at Eden Quay by an unruly anti-suffrage crowd until she found shelter in Liberty Hall. She also supported the protests that were held against the implementation of the Cat and Mouse Act in June of 1913 and spoke out against the forcible feeding of imprisoned suffragettes. At a meeting of the IWFL in September of that year, she talked of the three great movements in Ireland: suffrage, industrial and nationalist.

Constance was involved in the Dublin Lockout of 1913 and was something of a celebrity – the countess in the soup kitchen! In the same year, Constance's husband, Count de Markievicz, left for his home country and only returned to Ireland once, when he visited Constance as she lay dying.

Constance Markievicz. (© National Library of Ireland)

Their split seems amicable as they continued to correspond throughout her life.

In 1914, the IWFL held their Daffodil Day, a national day of celebration. There were several presentations and Constance teamed up with Kathleen Houston to act out a dramatisation of the story of Joan of Arc. She also performed at the Abbey Theatre with Maud Gonne.

By 1915, Constance was becoming more involved in the Labour movement. In a speech she gave to the IWFL, quoted in the *Irish Citizen*, she said, 'Take up your responsibilities and be prepared to go your own way depending for safety on your own courage, your own truth, and your own common sense, and not on the problematic chivalry of the men you may meet on the way. The two brilliant classes of women who follow this higher ideal are Suffragettes and the Trades Union or Labour women. In them lies the hope of the future'.[1]

By 1916, Constance was an officer in the ICA and the most prominent woman to fight in the Easter Rising. After a skirmish and standoff at St Stephen's Green, where Constance shot a British Army sniper, she was arrested and sentenced to death, which was later changed to life imprisonment on account of her gender. She was incarcerated in Mountjoy Jail but then moved to Aylesbury Prison in the UK until she was released in 1917, with other prisoners who were granted a general amnesty by the British government. On her return home, Constance embarked on a tour of Ireland, giving speeches in towns such as Listowel, Bantry, Trim, Clonakilty, Tralee, Clonmel and Waterford.

In 1918, Constance became the first woman elected to the British House of Commons, but she did not take up her seat. Constance was arrested in May 1918 for her anti-conscription activities. She was imprisoned in Holloway at the time but was an abstention MP, as were other members of Sinn Fein. Her fellow suffragettes in the IWFL had campaigned for her and were delighted with such an achievement. She went on to become a Labour minister in the Dail from April 1919 to January 1922.

Constance toured America from April to June 1922, under the auspices of the American Association for the Recognition of the Irish Republic. Her travelling companion was Kathleen Barry, sister of Kevin Barry who was executed for his part in an Irish Volunteers operation which resulted in the deaths of three British soldiers. It was a successful tour and Constance eventually returned to Ireland where she was active in her political life up until the time of her death.

W.B. Yeats immortalised Constance and her sister in his poem, 'In Memory of Eva Gore-Booth and Con Markievicz'. Constance died in 1927 after an illness put her in hospital and it is estimated that over 100,000 people paid their respects to her as she lay in the Rotunda Rooms. De Valera gave the funeral oration at her burial in Glasnevin Cemetery. Today, there is a bust of Constance in St Stephen's Green that shows her in her Citizen's Army uniform, overlooking the area where she fought and was second-in-command.

Somerville and Ross
Edith Somerville (1858—1949) and Violet Martin (1862—1915)

Somerville and Ross is the collective name of two second cousins, Edith Somerville and Violet Martin. Edith was born in Corfu where her father was stationed, but the family shortly moved to Drishane, Castletownsend, County Cork. Violet was reared in Ross, County Galway and they met for the first time when they were in their twenties. They both came from Protestant Ascendancy, Anglo-Irish families. The women were to become prolific writers and Violet used the pseudonym Martin Ross throughout their writing career.

Edith and Violet were both educated at Alexandra College, Dublin where suffrage talks were given by Anna Haslam and women's issues were a matter of great debate. It may have been here that they first encountered the need for women to fight for the vote and it was something that they took home with them to Cork.

The two cousins founded their own suffrage society, the Munster Women's Franchise League, in 1910, with Edith as the president. It was a non-militant regional group with around 500 members. Although the women did not take direct action for their cause, they worked diligently for the enfranchisement of women. Violet was vice-president and in 1913, their association affiliated itself with the IWSF along with other groups from around the country, including Belfast, Birr, Waterford, Limerick, Derry, Newry, Connaught and Bushmills.

The IWSLGA had a branch in Cork and they were perturbed by the setting up of a new group, feeling that the women should be members of their own society. The Munster Women's Franchise League (MWFL) considered themselves different to the IWSLGA and continued to fight for suffrage in their own way. Their members included Mary MacSwiney and Susanne Day – both writers who used the written word to publicise their cause – something that was increasingly important in order to disseminate information and gain support. During the struggle for woman's suffrage, Edith and Violet wrote to newspapers and journals expressing their views on women's rights and promoting the work of the MWFL and the suffrage movement. They would continue to be a writing partnership throughout their lives and wrote several books together, including *An Irish Cousin*, *The Real Charlotte* and *Naboth's Vineyard*. They are perhaps most famous for their short stories collected together in *Some Experiences*

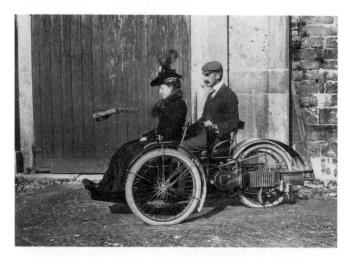

Violet Martin and companion. (© National Library of Ireland)

of an Irish R.M., *Further Experiences of an Irish R.M.* and *In Mr Knox's Country.*

The IWSLGA headquarters were in Cork but the women organised meetings around Munster, with Limerick being a common meeting place. The MWFL invited a Miss Abadam, president of the Beckenham branch of the NUWSS (UK), to speak at meetings in Cork and Limerick in 1913; when the meeting was disturbed in Cork with shots being fired, they had to ensure the meeting in Limerick was held behind closed doors and with a police presence.

Edith and Violet differed in their political ideals. Edith was a nationalist whilst Violet was a unionist, but they were both joined in the struggle for women's suffrage. Violet was happy to discuss her beliefs and often corresponded with the Galway MP, Stephen Gwynn, whose wife was also involved in the movement. Edith was asked to speak on behalf of the suffragettes at an Irish Convention by Sir Horace Plunkett, but she declined the invitation, preferring that someone else took the platform.

Violet died of a brain tumour in 1915, leaving Edith bereft but determined to continue their life's work, writing as Somerville and Ross. After Violet's death, Edith continued to publish novels and short stories and began attending séances where she felt she was in contact with Violet. Every evening she would allow herself to write automatically and believed that she could channel Violet's words, so that even in death these close companions and prolific writers could continue to work together.

In 1932, Edith was awarded the degree of Doctor of Letters by Trinity College Dublin. She was invited to join the Irish Academy of Letters by W.B. Yeats and in her later years was awarded the Gregory Gold Medal, the most prestigious literary award given by the academy. Edith died in 1949.

Isabella Tod
(1836–1896)

Isabella was one of the first women to spread the suffrage message in Ireland and the UK. Born in Edinburgh in 1836, she came from a Scots-Irish family. Her father, James Banks Tod, was a merchant who married Maria Waddell, a woman from County Monaghan with a strong Presbyterian background; the Revd Charles Masterton, a leading Presbyterian minister in seventeenth-century Belfast, was one of her ancestors. As a result, Isabella felt strongly about her faith and it was to influence her later life as a suffragette and female activist.

Isabella moved to Belfast with her parents when she was in her 20s. At around this time, she began writing anonymously for the *Dublin University Magazine* and *Banner of Ulster* and later the *Northern Whig* and the *Englishwomen's Review*.

As early as 1870, Isabella began organising suffrage meetings across the island from Cork to Belfast, some with Anna Robertson from Dublin. She spoke at countless suffrage events and meetings. In 1873, Isabella and a Miss Beedy toured Ireland with the suffrage message: starting in Belfast, travelling through Carrickfergus, Coleraine, Armagh, Dungannon, Derry and ending in Dublin. On 18 May 1878, Isabella was at the home of Mr and Mrs Hale in Eton College where she spoke about women's suffrage and in 1879, she was in Bristol speaking at the Bristol and West of England Society for Women's Suffrage annual general meeting. She addressed a meeting in April 1884 in Newcastle and by May she was at the Cambridge Working Men's Liberal Association with Millicent Fawcett. She spoke at a meeting in Gainsborough, Lincolnshire in 1885 along with Florence Balgarnie and Miss Taylour, and then in Rochdale, Lancashire at the Mechanics' Institute with Walter McLaren. Isabella travelled to Cheltenham, Exeter, Croydon, Dover, Glasgow and many other parts of England and Ireland to spread the message of women's rights and their right to vote.

In 1871, Isabella founded the North of Ireland Women's Suffrage Society or the IWSS acting as their secretary until the 1890s. It had close links to the London Women's Suffrage Society and lobbied in three main areas: the right to vote, municipal voting for women and the right for women to become Poor Law Guardians. The last two areas were accomplished in Isabella's lifetime, due at least in part to her efforts. She also became involved in the repeal of the Contagious Diseases Act, as many other early suffragettes were. Isabella became secretary of the Belfast branch of the Ladies National Association, which sought to stop the forced medical examinations that women deemed as prostitutes were subjected to.

Isabella made close connections with many suffragists of the times, including Millicent Fawcett, the leader of the NUWSS from 1890 to 1919. But Isabella was not always in favour; she did not agree with the Home Rule Bill that many suffragettes supported. It lost her friends and contacts, but she was adamant that Ireland should remain under British rule. She felt that to do otherwise was to destroy Ireland's economic base and went as far as sitting on the executive committee of the Ulster Women's Liberal Unionist Association that drew up a petition signed by 30,000 people and presented it to Queen Victoria, asking her not to agree to Home Rule.

In 1873, she was the first woman in Ireland to demand that women should be allowed education in universities. The following year, she published a paper entitled 'On advanced education for girls in the upper and middle classes' which had previously been presented to the National Association for the Promotion of Social Science. Isabella believed in a world where women had the right to education. In 1876, she helped to found the Belfast Ladies Institute, an institute that gave lectures to women on a range of subjects from history to modern languages. She was also instrumental in the formation of the Ulster Head Schoolmistresses Association in 1880, created to lobby government for changes to women's education.

Isabella didn't stop there. Her interests were many and so she invested her time and commitment in a variety of ways – all, however, worked to alleviate the plight of women and to raise their status through education and the right to participate in the political arena. In 1874, Isabella formed the Belfast Women's Temperance Association with Margaret Byers, another influential woman of the time. She spoke on the issue of temperance, seeing that if alcohol and drink-related issues were addressed it would improve the lives of women. The association set up eating houses in Belfast for girls who were working in the factories, to provide them with at least one healthy meal a day, and established a home for alcoholic women. Forty branches of the association could be found across Ireland and in 1894 these were merged into the Irish Women's Temperance Union. Isabella also became vice-president of the Irish Women's Total Abstinence Union in 1893 and held this position until her death.

In appreciation for all her work over the years, in 1884 Isabella was presented with a testimonial of £1,000 and in 1886 she received a full-length portrait. She spent her final years in ill-health but was still supporting causes up until her death in 1896, such as attending a meeting about the plight of the Armenian people. She died in her home at No. 71 Botanic Avenue, Belfast and did not live to see the women's vote accomplished. The mayoress of Belfast at the time said:

> She was one of the first to encourage the new movement of feminine emancipation which has developed so strikingly in our time ... In the political movement to which she devoted a great deal of time and energy – women's suffrage – she did not want the suffrage for its own sake, or the sake of any political power that might accrue, but because she considered it, to quote her own words, 'the only practical means of addressing many wrongs'.[1]

In March 2013, a blue plaque was erected on her house in Botanic Avenue, Belfast.

Jennie Wyse Power
(1858–1941)

Jennie was born Jane O'Toole at Baltinglass, County Wicklow in 1858 to Edward O'Toole and Mary (*née* Norton), both from farming families around the area. Jennie was one of seven children born in their house, which was on the main street where their father had a shop, trading in provisions and leather goods. In 1860, this business was sold and the family moved to Dublin where Edward continued trading until his death in 1876. Mary died just a year later.

Little is known of Jennie's whereabouts in her early years, but by 1881 she was embarking on her first move into the political arena. When Jennie joined the Ladies' Land League in that year, she met Anna Parnell, sister of Charles Stewart Parnell, who was to become a great influence in her life. The Ladies' Land League provided relief for evicted tenants, kept registers of landlords and their rents, and provided support to the leaders of the Irish National Land League when they were imprisoned in 1881. But in 1882 the organisation folded.

Jennie married John Wyse Power in 1883 and had four children, one of whom was named Charles Stewart after Parnell. Her husband was editor of the *Leinster Leader* newspaper, a member of the Irish Republican Brotherhood and a founder member of the Gaelic Athletic Association (GAA). Their daughter, Nancy Wyse Power, was also extremely active as a nationalist and member of Cumman na mBan.

Jennie was a member of the DWSA in her early years and stayed with them during their change to the IWSLGA. For Jennie, there were two struggles: that of a free Ireland and an Ireland where women could vote and be involved in the political life of their country.

In 1899, Jennie set up business at No. 21 Henry Street with her shop, the Irish Farm Produce Company, selling all Irish produce including eggs, butter, cream, honey and confectionery. It also had a restaurant, and it was from here that meals were sent to convicted suffragettes. The restaurant became a meeting place for prominent nationalists and was the site of the signing of the Proclamation of the Irish Republic in April 1916. In 1908, Jennie expanded her business with further premises in Lower Camden Street.

The plaque at 21 Henry Street. (© J.R. Webb)

As well as being an astute businesswoman, Jennie became more involved in the nationalist struggle. Inghinidhe na hÉireann (Daughters of Ireland) was formed in 1900 as an autonomous all-female organisation and was led by the radical Maud Gonne, with Jennie listed as its vice-president in its 1901 annual report. Its aim was to promote cultural nationalism and its members later merged into the Cumman na mBan. Inghinidhe na hÉireann was instrumental in setting up a Patriotic Children's Treat in response to a previously held Children's Treat which was part of Queen Victoria's visit to Dublin. The nationalist movement were against the queen's visit and its aim to enlist Irishmen in the British Army to fight the Boer War. The Patriotic Children's Treat differed in that it promoted nationalism and included anti-recruitment speeches as well as a picnic for over 30,000 children from the more patriotic families.

In 1903, Jennie was elected as a Poor Law Guardian in North Dublin and she remained in this role for eight years, working to ameliorate poor social conditions. Jennie also became an active member of Sinn Féin and in 1908 she was elected to its executive committee. She attended the meeting in Dublin in June 1912, to demand that women's suffrage was added to the Home Rule Bill, along with Constance de Markievicz, Kathleen Lynn and other trade union and nationalist women. Jennie told the assembled crowd:

> The Sinn Féin Party, to which I belong, passed unanimously a resolution in favour of votes for women, and as an Irish nationalist I cannot see why there should be any antagonism between the Irish women's demand for citizenship and the demand for a native parliament. Our claim is that we shall not be debarred merely by sex from the rights of citizens.[1]

Jennie was involved in a protest meeting held in Dublin to mark the arrival of Asquith, the UK's prime minister, that turned sour for all the women involved. Speeches were given by Margaret Cousins and Margaret Connery from the IWFL and Mrs Chambers from the IWSS, Belfast, but they were drowned out by the calls of an organised crowd believed to be from the Ancient Order of Hibernians. As the women tried to leave they were attacked, their clothes torn and stones thrown at them. Jennie was caught up in this wild and vicious assault that left the women bruised and beaten.

This was a difficult time for women who were both nationalists and suffragists. Jennie tried to heal the rift that had grown between them by writing in the *Irish Independent*:

> Nationalist women refrained from placing their suffrage views before the Irish Parliamentary Party while that party was carrying the Home Rule Bill through the English House of Commons. Now, however, the situation has quite changed, and those of us who are Irish Nationalists can only hope that an appeal at this time to the extension of the suffrage to Irishwomen will not fall on unheeding ears.[2]

In 1914, Jennie became a founder member of Cumann na mBan, initially the female offshoot of the Irish Volunteers, and was especially active in its Central Branch which met every Thursday in Rutland Square. When Cumann na mBan was reorganised in 1915, Jennie took the role of president. The women involved with this organisation were some of the most politically active of the time: the women who fought for their nationality and freedom from British rule. They were the backbone behind the Easter Rising and were instrumental in the creation of the new Irish Republic. Although many of the women had close friendships during these times, Jennie had an especially close bond with Constance de Markievicz who moved into her home in Henry Street just before the Easter Rising, as did Kathleen Lynn.

In the Easter Rising of 1916, Jennie's Henry Street shop was destroyed by fire, causing the family to lose their home and their livelihood. Further tragedy was to unfold when Maire, Jennie's oldest surviving daughter, died at just 28 years of age. However, the family home and premises was gradually rebuilt and by 1919 a room in her restaurant became the meeting place of the Irish Volunteers.

Jennie, although firmly placed in the Nationalist movement, continued her work for women's suffrage and in 1916 she also joined the IWFL, a more militant group than the IWSLGA. In 1917, she sat on their committee but also remained involved in the IWSLGA which was still headed by Anna Haslam.

Jennie's close friend, Constance de Markievicz, was elected as a parliamentary representative of Sinn Féin at the 1918 general election after Jennie and other members of Cumann na mBan, the IWWU, and the IWFL had vigorously campaigned for her. It was a huge achievement for all the women involved who, for the first time, were able to use their vote in a parliamentary election. In 1919, Jennie was appointed treasurer of the Sinn Féin Executive and was elected as one of five women members to sit on the Dublin Corporation board in 1920 for the Inns Quay–Rotunda District.

Jennie had always supported the Home Rule Bill and later the Anglo-Irish Treaty against many of her nationalist compatriot's wishes. In 1922, she helped set up Cumann na Saoirse (The League for Freedom) and spoke at its inaugural meeting with other pro-treaty activists. Her involvement in Cumann na Saoirse led to her support of the new political party, Cumann na nGaedhael, that was set up by the pro-treaty members of the Dail and led to Jennie becoming a senator in 1922.

Jennie was a member of the Senate from 1922 to 1936: first representing Cumann na nGaedhael then as an Independent and later as a member of Fianna Fáil. She continued to champion women's rights with her input into issues, such as allowing women to obtain the higher grades in the civil service and opposing the exclusion of women from jury service. She contributed to debates around the homeless, the poor and infant mortality, always fighting for the less fortunate. Jennie finally retired when she was 78, after years of being a major advocate for women's suffrage and an active member of the Nationalist movement.

Jennie died in 1941 and is buried in Glasnevin Cemetery. In 1991, a plaque was erected at No. 21 Henry Street by the 1916–21 Club to mark her premises and the site where the infamous proclamation was signed.

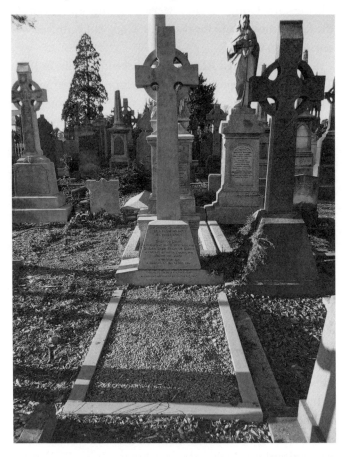

The resting place of Jennie Wyse Power at Glasnevin Cemetery. (© J.R. Webb)

Kathleen Lynn
(1874–1955)

Kathleen Florence Lynn was born near Killala, County Mayo in 1874. Her father, Robert Lynn, had attended Trinity College to study divinity while her mother, Katharine, was descended from planters granted lands in the Leitrim/Sligo area. She was one of four children who lived in Mullafarry, Shrule and Cong as they were growing up. In 1886, the family moved into the rectory in Cong but Kathleen was sent away to school.

Kathleen attended Alexandra College in Dublin in 1891. The school was a pioneering establishment that promoted women's education and rights and as such had strong links to the suffrage movement. Anna Haslam, who founded the DWSA, later to become the IWSLGA, was a close friend of Anne Jellicoe, the founder of the college, and so visited regularly, giving lectures and encouraging the girls to discuss issues of women's rights and suffrage. From this introduction into the women's movement, Kathleen was later to join the IWSLGA and the WSPU based in London.

In 1899, Kathleen graduated from the Royal University of Ireland as a doctor and continued her studies in the US, gaining a postgraduate degree. In 1903, she moved to Rathmines, sharing her home with her lifelong partner Madeline ffrench-Mullen and it was in Rathmines that she set up her own GP practice in 1904. By 1909, she was a fellow of the Royal College of Surgeons and her medical career had taken off.

In 1911, Kathleen joined Delia in her work for the IWWU and became their vice-president. Kathleen attended the mass meeting of 1912 where women gathered to demand that suffrage was included in the Home Rule Bill. During the lockout of 1913, she worked as a medical officer and was present at the food kitchen in Liberty Hall to monitor daily rations and nutritional requirements of the locked out workers and their children. In 1913, she also became the medical examiner to imprisoned suffragettes along with Kathleen Maguire and was appalled by what she saw. In 1914, she spoke to the Church League for Women's Suffrage on the effects of force feeding and on her experience as a doctor to the suffragettes in Mountjoy Jail. Kathleen was a Protestant and believed that the Church could be doing more for women's suffrage. She presented the Dean of St Patrick's Cathedral with a petition signed by over 1,300 members of the Church of Ireland to ask for the churches support for women's suffrage in prayer and in services, but this was denied.

Kathleen had been involved in the Irish Citizen Army (ICA) mostly to give first-aid classes but 1916 saw a division in her loyalties. She was working for the Royal Victoria Eye and Ear Hospital (RVEEH) whose role was to treat wounded British soldiers, but she was also chief medical officer for the ICA. Stopping at the City Hall Garrison with medical supplies, she was confronted with the dying ICA captain, Sean Connolly. Kathleen tried in vain to save his life and stayed with the small band of ICA fighters until they were surrounded. As chief medical officer she was the next highest-ranking officer and it was Kathleen herself who gave the surrender to the British Army.

She was taken to Kilmainham Jail along with Constance de Markievicz, Madeline ffrench-Mullen and Helena Moloney, and then moved to Mountjoy. Her involvement resulted in her dismissal from the RVEEH and made it difficult for her to find work in any other hospital. Kathleen's father disowned her after her involvement in the troubles of 1916 and they did not begin patching up their relationship until 1920.

Cumann na dTeachtaire (or the League of Women's Delegates) was formed by members of Cumaan na mBan, the ICA, Inghinidhe na hÉireann and the IWWU in 1917, to organise women to attend all nationalist conferences and to ensure that women's rights and suffrage remained on the political agenda. Kathleen became an active member and continued to work for women's suffrage and the Nationalist movement.

In 1917 Kathleen, with Constance de Markievicz, Kathleen Clarke and Grace Plunkett, joined the executive of Sinn Fein. Her involvement in Sinn Fein was seen as a threat to the British government and she spent weeks on the run, then endured constant raids at her house when at home. Throughout all this time, however, she still treated wounded patients and continued to practice medicine wherever she could.

Kathleen was one of the women who used their vote for the first time in the 1918 general election, but the suffrage movement still had far to go. This vote only applied to women over 30 years of age who owned certain property or passed other qualifications, but it was still a victory for all the women who had been fighting for their right to vote.

The global flu pandemic of 1918 interrupted Kathleen's political activism for a time. It was an especially lethal pandemic as it affected healthy adults, and it is estimated that some 500 million people were killed across the globe. Inoculation was rare and there were no antibiotics, but Kathleen and her colleagues worked tirelessly to immunize and treat people and children from a temporary flu clinic they set up in Charlemont Street. Babies began to arrive and Kathleen had to take in a motherless baby as there was no children's hospital. Kathleen saw the need for a specific place for children to be treated and so co-founded St Ultan's Children Hospital in Dublin with Madeline ffrench-Mullen in 1919. To begin with, it catered for babies up to the age of 1, which was later stretched to 2 and children up to the age of 5 could be treated as outpatients. Many of the staff at St Ultan's were the women that Kathleen had taught through the ICA and her other political affiliations.

In her later years, St Ultan's became her life's work as she became more disillusioned with the political environment. Yet Kathleen still had time to be active in the Women's Prisoners'

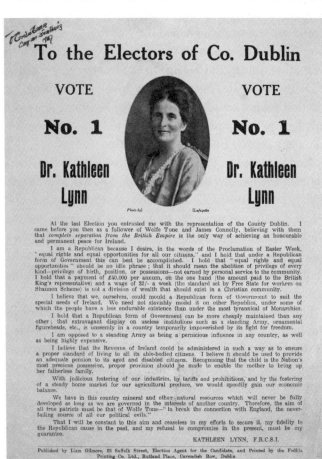

Dr Kathleen Lynn's election flyer. (© National Library of Ireland)

Defence League. This group, established by Maud Gonne, was known as the 'Mothers' and aimed to raise awareness of the plight of over 400 female prisoners that had been imprisoned by the new Free State government. Letters were sent to the press and public rallies were organised. The 'Mothers' protested on the streets against the women's incarceration, even though they were doused with water and shot at.

Kathleen took part in celebrations when, in 1922, the Irish Free State constitution granted the vote to men and women over 21 years of age. In 1923, she ran in the elections with four other women and became one of forty-four abstention TDs in the Dáil. Abstentionism involved standing for election but not actually taking a seat or becoming any more involved with the proceedings of running government – a strategy used by Irish nationalist parties.

Kathleen died in 1955 and was still working in St Ultan's up until five months before her death. She had led the way with her use of the BCG vaccination some ten years before it was in general use across the country. She also promoted the work of Maria Montessori whom she met in 1934 and went on to establish a Montessori ward in St Ultan's. When she died, nurses lined the route her coffin took as it passed the hospital she had both founded and given her life to.

She was awarded full military honours at her burial with the ICA forming her guard of honour. A bugler sounded the last post and members of the 7th Eastern Battalion fired three volleys over her grave. She is buried at Deansgrange with her mother, sister and brother.

Mary Colum
(1884–1957)

Mary was born Mary Gunning Maguire in Collooney, County Sligo, daughter of Charles and Catherine, and one of five children. Mary's family was middle class and Catholic, and her father worked for the Royal Irish Constabulary. Mary lost her mother when she was young and was subsequently raised by her grandmother in Ballisodare, also in Sligo. She was sent to St Louis' Convent in Monaghan and continued her studies at the National University of Ireland where she studied literature. During this time she helped to start the Twilight Literary Society, a group who often frequented the Abbey Theatre, taking part in literary debates and attending events where the writers of the day met.

After her graduation in 1908, Mary's love of literature and language led her to teach modern languages at Scoil Ite (St Ita's), the school established by Mary MacSwiney and her sister, Annie. During her time here, Mary helped found the *Irish Review* which was to establish her literary career. In 1910, Mary was amongst the crowds who had gathered to see Mrs Pankhurst speak about the fight for women's right to vote. She became a member of the IWFL and attended many meetings along with her husband, Padraic Colum. She married Padraic, a poet and playwright, whose work was performed at the Abbey Theatre in 1912. The Colums were close friends of Margaret and James Cousins and became interested in the suffrage movement through their regular discussions. Padraic took up the role of joint editor of the *Irish Review* and Mary wrote several articles concerning the suffrage movement for this publication, as well as publishing articles from suffragettes such as Hanna Sheehy Skeffington.

Mary was interested in both the suffrage and nationalist movements. She was a member of Cumann na mBan and acted as an honorary secretary along with Louise Gavan Duffy. The women had met when they were teaching in St Enda's, Patrick Pearse's school in Rathmines. Mary believed that helping the Irish Volunteers was necessary, patriotic work and although suffrage was important, nationalism was more so. For Mary, Cumann na mBan was an independent body with its own executive and constitution and not just a part of the Irish Volunteers or 'camp-followers' as some had suggested.

On 26 July 1914, the Colum's were involved in the Howth gunrunning plot. Arms were needed for the Irish Volunteers to use in their rebellion and ultimately for the Easter Rising in 1916. Around 1,500 rifles were purchased in Germany and shipped to Howth on the *Asgard*. Constance de Markievicz and members of the Irish Citizen Army met the boat with handcarts and wheelbarrows to transport the rifles away. The Harbour Master informed the authorities and they were met by British troops. As they kept them talking, the men and women at the rear of the group spirited away the rifles and only three of the 1,500 were found.

Soon after their part in the gunrunning plot, Mary and Padraic moved to America where they lived most of their lives and focused on their writing. During Mary's life she wrote over 100 articles and reviews for various publications like *Scribner's Magazine*, the *Tribune* and the *New York Herald*. Mary was lauded as a top-notch critic and an authority on literature. She had begun to make her name through her work with the *Irish Review* but, on emigrating to America, she continued to mix in literary circles and to write essays and criticisms on the top writers of the day. She may have been a critic but she was also friendly with many of the writers she reviewed, including W.B. Yeats, Maxwell Perkins, Elinor Wylie, Amy Lowell, Sherwood Anderson and James Joyce. She was particularly close to Joyce who often spent hours with Mary and her husband, debating the issues of the day and the way in which their writing could reflect them. After her death in 1957, Padraic put together her memoir 'Our Friend James Joyce' for publication.

In 1922, the couple returned to Ireland but moved back to the USA and settled in Connecticut in 1925. They also lived in France for a time before finally settling on New York as their home town. From here, Mary and Padraic both taught literature at Columbia University.

In 1937, Mary's book *From These Roots: The Ideas That Have Made Modern Literature* was published by Scribner's and Sons after a Guggenheim Fellowship made her research possible. Mary also wrote an account of her early years in *Dublin, Life and the Dream*, which was published in 1947. It gives us great insight into turn-of-the-century Dublin, a young woman's experience of studying at university and the intellectual pleasures it brought her amidst the backdrop of an Ireland in political turmoil.

Mary spent her life writing and adding to the debate on nationalism and the suffrage movement through the medium of the written word. After her death, she was returned home to be buried in St Fintan's Cemetery, Dublin. Padraic was also buried here after his death in 1972.

Marion Duggan (1885–1943)

Marion Elizabeth Duggan was born in County Westmeath around 1885 and her father, James, worked for the Bank of Ireland. When Marion was 16 she was living in Borris, County Offaly but by 1911, she was living with her mother and father in Mander's Terrace, Rathmines. Marion studied logic and ethics at Trinity College, graduating in 1908, and was awarded an LLB in 1910. She was to use her knowledge of law and justice to further the causes that she was interested in.

Marion disagreed with direct militancy; her views were much more pacifist and socialist. Much of her commitment was to the IWRL, formed in 1911, which she believed had a better chance of achieving the vote through constitutional reform than by direct action. When the league formed a committee to monitor court cases involving women, she wrote frequent reports that appeared in the *Irish Citizen* under the column 'In the Courts'.

In April 1913, Marion wrote an article entitled, 'Are Militants Suffragists?' and contributed to an ongoing debate between militant and constitutional suffragists as to whose methods were best. In it she says:

> Readers of the last two numbers of the *Irish Citizen* will readily understand that I was keenly interested in the article, entitled 'A Holy War', which appeared in last week's issue. It told me so many things about my own views I never knew before! There was, however, just one trifle which the author no doubt advertently omitted to make clear. It is a small point, but without some explanation I find great difficulty in answering her. It is this: Do militants believe that women should have votes; or, in other words, do they hold that the women who suffragists propose to entrust with the Parliamentary Franchise, are capable today of making an intelligent use thereof? The 'militant movement' started to secure votes for women, and loudly its teachers declared women were fit to vote; but on reading 'A Christian Militant's' personal opinion (by the way militants say they never abuse constitutionalists!) I cannot really believe that she thinks 'one who discloses an excusable and appalling ignorance', 'a dishonest distortion of facts', 'a blind leader of the blind' etc, is fit to vote on questions of national importance. My views are those of the National Union of Women Suffrage Societies, and the Labour Party, who must, therefore be equally guilty and equally unreliable. It is a pity, because the man in the street reading such an article, and the similar one by Miss Pankhurst in the 'Suffragette' of 21st March 1913, will have no doubt come to the conclusion that as the militants believe constitutionalists morally dead, they do not intend to cease from militancy upon the enfranchisement of the morally dead. I was recently told that 'many

people' believe that had it not been for militancy, the Liberal women would never have insisted upon the passing into law of the White Slave Traffic Bill, i.e., that without militancy an educated body of women, knowing all the facts of this diabolical trade, would have done nothing to put an effective end to it!

Therefore, you must worry them into it! It is an intelligent theory, but you can't call it suffrage. It brings home the necessity of declaring non-militant societies anti-militant. It supposes that had we been enfranchised in 1910, militancy would still be required to rouse women voters in 1912. It is necessary to keep non-militants up to the mark. Mr Maurice Wilkins makes a really fine defence of 'militancy', but both critics make the mistake of substituting the particular for the general. 'All humanity got a trumpet call to militancy'. Pillarbox outrages are militancy. Therefore, humanity got a trumpet-call to destroy letters. Every form of spirited protest must be tried. This is exactly where 'A Christian Militant' and I part company. She holds that the need to wage 'a holy war' justifies any weapon, except possibly murder. I do not.[1]

Marion was never shy of writing her point of view and using the written word to address women's rights issues. She was a pioneer in reporting on domestic violence, child abuse and crimes against women, exposing the courts for their treatment of sexual crime and calling for reform. One of her reports produced in the *Irish Citizen* includes the cases the IWRL were watching, and also underlines why they felt this necessary:

Two cases involving sexual offences against little girls were before Mr Hunt in the Northern Police Court on Monday, June 29th, and have been returned for trial at City Sessions on 9th July.

John Madden, a 'free labourer', now an ice-cream vendor, is alleged to have attempted to assault a child aged six years and eleven months in Lower Gardiner Street. Dr Boyd Barrett deposed that the victim is suffering from venereal disease (gonorrhoea). Bail refused. A Protestant clergyman is said to have gone bail in £20 for a man named Jones, resident in Drumcondra, who is accused of indecent conduct towards an eight-year-old girl.

It will be remembered that the Irishwomen's Reform League, some months ago, resolved to take action with view to bringing before the notice of the Court their desire that such cases should be punished with the utmost severity.

Accordingly, Messrs. Cochrane & Co., 18 Harcourt Street, have been instructed to hold a Watching Brief on our behalf, and in Madden's case we trust the Court will not deny that we have a right to be interested in the proceedings. We have in hand a number of subscriptions towards the expense, but more are needed. We trust that those who feel that children ought to be protected from human beasts will try to spare us a trifle.

It must be clearly understood that: (1) A refusal to allow our representative to speak will not necessarily mean that our trouble has been for nothing. (2) We are not out to try and force the conviction of innocent men; but merely to assist in getting at the truth and to voice the 'women's point of view', in order that sympathy with the prisoner will not lead to a short sentence. (3) We do not propose to be represented in every case, but will, if allowed, intervene from time to time, in order to create a strong public opinion and to prevent secrecy. (4) There is a need for our urging stern measures …[2]

Marion was also heavily involved with the Irish Women's Workers Union and at one point took over the running of the IWWU until she handed over the reins to Louie Bennett. She contributed to the labour movement, moving in the same circles as Jennie Wyse Power, Kathleen Lynn and Elizabeth Bloxham. She was also a member of the Central Committee for Women's Employment for the Provinces of Leinster, Munster and Connaught.

Marion died in Dublin in 1943 after a lifetime of fighting for justice and women's rights.

Mary MacSwiney
(1872–1942)

Mary was born in London in 1872 to an Anglo-Irish Catholic family. Her father was John MacSwiney, a teacher in the UK and later, the owner of a tobacco company in Cork. Returning to Ireland when she was 6, she was later educated at St Angela's Ursuline High School in Cork. She studied for a teaching diploma at Cambridge University and taught in schools in the UK. When her mother, Mary (*née* Wilkinson), died she returned to Cork to look after her younger siblings. Her father had emigrated to Australia in 1885 when his business had failed. In 1911, she was living in Blackrock as head of the family with her brothers, Sean and Terence.

Back at home, she joined the Munster Women's Franchise League but she was later to leave the non-party, non-sectarian society due to her Nationalist feelings and the fact that the MWFL had decided to support the British at war. Tellingly, she was one of the women who signed a statement denouncing the British suffragettes who had attacked the British Prime Minister, Asquith, on Irish soil. Mary was to become very vocal on her opposition to British suffragettes trying to take over the Irish cause. The final straw was when the MFWL bought an ambulance to donate to the British military and Mary, although supporting the suffrage movement, wanted to do more from a nationalist standpoint.

Mary was a member of Inghinidhe na hÉireann and Cumman na mBan and became the latter association's vice-president. She established the Cork branch of Cumann na mBan in 1914 and was arrested for her part in the 1916 Easter Rising. Mary had moved from suffrage to nationalism, but tried to support both causes and encouraged others to do so. Not everyone was convinced by her arguments. Mary's unhappiness with suffragettes and the suffrage movement that did not place nationalism as their priority was played out in the pages of the *Irish Citizen*. On 2 May 1914, she wrote:

> I wish to protest in the most emphatic manner against the remarks made in your Current Comment recently about those Irish women who consider that in the present crisis their country's interests must come first. You cannot be ignorant that that attitude is adopted by the vast majority of Nationalist suffragists. Are you so totally devoid of common-sense – not to speak of political acumen – that you cannot discriminate between the attitude of Nationalist women in Ireland and Party women in England? To characterise our point of view as 'slavish' and a display of 'crawl-servility to men' is the very best anti-suffragist campaign you can carry on in this country ... If you continue at the present rate alienating Nationalist opinion from the Suffrage cause, I should advise you to use a subtitle for your paper – Chief Anti-Suffragist Organ in Ireland.[1]

The debate continued through correspondence for several days but on 23 May, the *Irish Citizen* did publish a longer article written by Mary, albeit with the comment that 'we publish this week another of those wrong-headed appeals by which Miss MacSwiney, the spokeswoman of the Slave Women (Nationalist variety) seeks to justify her placing of a party Nationalism above the cause of her sex.'[2]

This war of words serves to show just how complex the fight for the female vote in Ireland was against the political background of the times. Mary said:

> To plead with suffragists for a little common sense and political insight may be looked upon nowadays as a request for a dispatch of

coals to Newcastle, and yet it seems to be true that many Irish suffragists are rather losing their heads, and by their present tactics injuring their own cause. This does not apply to Militants only, but to all those who views are expressed in recent 'leaders' of the Irish Citizen. In England, convinced suffragists rightly place Votes for Women above and before all other reforms, and this policy expresses itself in consistent and continual opposition to the Government, while the Government, as such, is opposed to Women's Suffrage. No question of party – no reform of any kind – social, fiscal, agrarian – can in any way compare with the dominant need in England today – the Woman's Voice – backed by the power of the Vote – in all questions of reform. But in Ireland, even those who place suffrage first must take the special circumstances of the country into consideration if they wish to win adherents to their cause. Ireland's struggling to settle not a Party question, but a National one, and opposition to the Government in the present crisis means opposition to Home Rule.

The fact that many Irish suffragists play the political ostrich and refuse to recognise the essential difference between this and English Party questions, does not minimise that difference; it simply blinds their political intelligence and injures the cause they wish to promote ...[3]

In 1916, Mary lost her teaching position when she was arrested for her part in the Easter Rising. She decided to keep teaching and established Scoil Ite's School for Girls in Wellington Road, Cork, with her sister, Annie. Mary always refused to take any money from the Department of Education for the running of her school and ensured that Irish culture and language was key to the curriculum. Mary was to be involved with her school throughout her lifetime. At its closure in 1954, many of the pupils transferred to a school still in operation today.

Mary's brother, Terence, whom she had raised in Blackrock, was Lord Mayor of Cork, a member of the

IRA and a writer. He was arrested on suspicion of having seditious documents in 1920 and sent to Brixton Prison, where he went on hunger strike for seventy-four days before he died. After his death, Mary gave evidence to the American Commission on 'Conditions in Ireland' in Washington DC. Her writing at the time 'The Background of the Irish Republic' was later published by the Benjamin Franklin Bureau. Mary toured the US with Terence's widow, Muriel, speaking on the War of Independence and rallying support and publicity for the nationalist cause.

After a long, drawn-out custody battle, Mary became joint guardian of her brother Terence's daughter, Maire, and brought her home to Cork amidst much secrecy. Maire would grow up to marry Ruairi Brugha, son of Cathal Brugha, the politician and revolutionary who was shot dead in 1922 during the Civil War.

Mary was twice imprisoned during Ireland's time of civil unrest and underwent a twenty-one-day hunger strike when she was in Mountjoy Jail. She also took part in a twenty-four-hour hunger strike when she was incarcerated in Kilmainham Jail. Her sister, Annie, when refused permission to see her, sat outside the prison gates and undertook a hunger strike too, in support of her sister.

In 1921, Mary had gained a seat for Sinn Fein in the Dail for the Cork Borough constituency. She kept her seat during the 1923 general elections but then refused to take up her position in line with the reaction of other Sinn Fein members. Mary violently opposed the Anglo-Irish Treaty and was to remain a Nationalist all her life. She has been remembered for many of her rousing speeches, one over three hours long, which she gave, calling for the freedom of Ireland.

She died at home in Cork in 1942.

Susanne Rouviere Day
(1876–1964)

Susanne was born in Cork at Sidney Place in 1876 to a Protestant family. Her parents were Robert, a prominent Cork businessman, and Rebecca Day (*née* Scott). Susanne's father was involved in the Cork Historical and Archaeological Society and had a keen interest in artefacts and collecting antiques. In 1901, Susanne was living with her mother, father, brother, William and niece and nephew in Ballinamough West. By 1911, the household had been reduced to just Susanne and her parents living at No. 1 Lover's Walk in Cork.

Susanne helped to establish the Munster Women's Franchise League with Edith Somerville and Violet Martin, and became its secretary. She was also a member of the Irishwomen's Suffrage Federation, travelling around the country to talk about suffrage at various meetings and helping to set up branches of the MWFL in Waterford, Nenagh, Tralee and Limerick. She was also involved in the Cork branch of the IWFL which ran counter to the non-militant stance of the MWFL, but Susanne was a pacifist at heart and would not become involved in direct action, preferring to use her pen as a weapon.

In 1911, Susanne became Cork's first female poor law guardian. Women were allowed to sit on Poor Law Boards from 1896 and their role was to assess the situation of the poor in their area and make improvements as to their welfare. Susanne found the role difficult and challenging, something she addressed in her writings.

Susanne was primarily a writer and was to make her mark with several pieces of work, including her pamphlet 'Women in the New Ireland: Why Irishwomen Need the Vote', published in 1912 on behalf of the MWFL.

In September 1913, she told readers of the *Irish Citizen* about her suffragette tour around Kerry. It starts:

> The campaign opened in Cahirciveen on Tuesday night, when the Carnegie Hall was filled with an audience which listened intently to the speeches. No need to drive home the principles of liberty and emancipation in the town which gave birth to Daniel O'Connell! The speakers were on sure ground, and as point after point was raised and emphasised, it was encouraging to see men and women, who had lounged carelessly back in their seats at first, lean forward now eager to catch every word of this newest phase on the emancipation of Irish People.
>
> From Cahirciveen we went to Waterville where, owing to difficulties connected with the halls, we had to speak in the open air to a crowd composed of fishermen, shopkeepers, farmers and farm labourers, telegraphists from the cable station, and English visitors. It was not an easy matter to pitch a speech in a key to ring harmoniously over such a mixed assemblage, but the meeting was held principally for the inhabitants, so we spoke directly to them. Here again, we were received with the utmost courtesy and interest, and the constant 'that's true' and 'you're right' showed how the points went home.

Susanne continues to describe her tour, including a visit to Valencia Island, Killorglin, and Tralee. When in Killorglin, she says:

> ... there was the largest crowd. A thick mass of men and women standing at the back, and the chairs filled, with the exception of the front row. They inclined to be facetious at first, and 'out for a lark' many of them. A few trenchant remarks on the labour question, the importance of the vote for working women, and its benefits through them to working men, soon caught their attention, and in spite of an element in the audience which might easily have spoiled it, the meeting was one of the best we held. One or two attempted interruptions were put down with a firm hand by those who had come

> to listen. The inevitable 'local celebrity' sat prominently in the front row, shouting his approbation, but a quiet 'please don't interrupt' from the platform was taken in good part, and he too, composed himself to listen. One determined reactionary, also in the front row, informed us several times that we should be at home ...[1]

In 1912, Susanne also had articles published in the *Irish Review* on 'The crime called outdoor relief' and 'The workhouse child'. She is perhaps most remembered for her work, *The Amazing Philanthropist*: being extracts from the letters of Lester Martin, an account of her experiences and challenges as a poor law guardian told through the medium of fictionalised letters. Published in 1916, it scandalised some of her peers who saw it as an attack on poor law guardianship and relief work. However, it also contained a closer look at the suffrage movement and how people in rural Cork reacted to it, thinking that the women were immoral and degenerate. It gives us a snapshot of how brave the women were who took the suffrage message around Ireland against a prevailing public attitude.

As well as writing about her political views and firmly supporting the suffrage cause, Susanne also wrote successful plays, most notably those written with Geraldine Cummins, a fellow suffragist. Two of their plays, *Broken Faith* and *Fox and Geese* were performed at the Abbey Theatre in Dublin. She also had her own work produced and wrote a play for the IWRL in 1914 entitled *Toilers*.

Susanne went to live in France in 1916 but returned to Cork to live in Myrtle Hill House after her mother's death. Later, she moved to London to live near her friend, Geraldine Cummings, during the Second World War. During this time, some of her plays were shown at the Gaiety Theatre in Manchester.

She died in London in 1964.

Helen Chenevix
(1886–1963)

Helen was born in Blackrock in 1886 to Henry Chenevix and Charlotte (*née* Ormsby). Her father was a bishop in the Church of Ireland. She was educated at Alexandra College and would have encountered Anna Haslam during her time there and been introduced to lively debates about women's rights and the struggle to obtain the vote. She graduated from Trinity College in the first wave of women to obtain degrees, politicised even by her own actions.

In 1911, she was living with her parents in Pembroke West, Dublin and it was in this year that she helped to set up the IWSF with Louie Bennett. It marked the start of a lifelong friendship. The federation they established joined together several suffrage groups from around the country, acting as an umbrella organisation in the hope that placing the women together would negate discord and show a unified front. Helen was to take the role of joint honorary secretary with Louie and share the organisational running of the federation. In 1913, Helen was the federation's delegate, sent to a conference at Caxton Hall in the UK, to discuss the implications of the Cat and Mouse Act as well as other suffrage concerns.

Helen was also instrumental in establishing the IWRL. The IWRL was originally formed as a Dublin branch of the IWSF but it was envisioned that it would work towards women's rights in general rather than just for women's votes. It was non-militant but did not stop its members, as individuals, from taking part in direct action if they wished. As a member of this organisation, Helen wrote to the Lord Lieutenant of Ireland to discontinue the use of the Cat and Mouse Act in Belfast and she spoke at many meetings regarding the suffrage issue and concerns surrounding the lack of women's rights in Ireland.

Helen took the platform at the mass meeting of suffragettes in June 1912, along with Delia Larkin, to rally support for women's suffrage. Delia became a close friend of hers and was to work with her on many issues in later years.

In 1916, Helen helped Louie Bennett to set up the IWWU along with Delia and Hanna Sheehy Skeffington. In 1918, the IWWU was officially recognised as a trade union and had over 5,000 members. They operated from Liberty Hall in Dublin and sought to challenge poor working conditions for women and to negotiate with their employers. They also sought wage increases and set holiday periods. It was the only union solely representative of women at the time and covered a wide range of issues pertaining to girls and women in the workforce. In 1927, Helen, along with Louie, spoke to the *Saorstát Éireann* technical education commission on raising the school leaving age of girls from 14 to 16, and including girls in agricultural schools as well as providing training for girls going into domestic service. The work of the IWWU was Helen's focus for many years.

Much has been made of Helen and Louie's relationship. They were constant companions and some have wondered if they were more than that. The women lived side by side for over twenty-five years; Louie bought a house next to Helen's in Killiney after receiving an inheritance on her mother's death. They also lived together for a time, with Helen caring for Louie during the illness that led to her death in 1956. Whatever their personal relationship, they had shared a close companionship that had seen them both working in political arenas for the advancement of women, especially through the IWWU and the IWRL.

Helen was elected to the Dublin Corporation and served as acting Lord Mayor of Dublin in 1942 and 1950. She was on the executive of the Irish Trade Union Congress from

1946–56 and served as president in 1951, one of only three women ever to hold that position. Helen also became the IWWU's General Secretary after Louie's retirement and subsequent death from 1955–1957.

She was a pacifist and, like many other suffragettes, became a member of the WILPF, also working with Louie during this time. The WILPF began as the Woman's Peace Party. It was a non-profit and non-governmental organisation set up in America in January 1915 that worked to unite women across the world in making known the causes of war and working towards a permanent peace. It eventually set up its headquarters in Geneva, Switzerland and in 1925 the Irish branch of the organisation invited the league to have its Fifth International Congress in Dublin the following year. Helen sat on the executive of the Irish League with Louie, Rosamund Jacob, Lucy Kingston and seven others and organised the congress to be held in the National University buildings in July 1926. Over 150 delegates representing twenty different countries attended for a week and it was an amazing success, the first international meeting held since

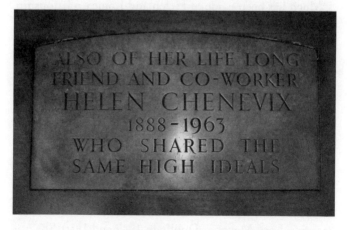

Plaque in honour of Helen Chenevix. (© J.R. Webb)

Ireland became a Free State. Helen's work for peace didn't stop there and she went on to be the vice-president of the Irish Pacifist Movement. Helen worked tirelessly throughout her life for women's rights, better working conditions for the women of Ireland and the right to live in a peaceful world, free of war. She continued her work until her death in Dublin in 1963.

Dora Mellone
(1872–?)

Dora was born in Wiltshire, England, the daughter of Presbyterian minister Revd W.E. Mellone and his wife, Elizabeth. The family lived in Kent before moving to Warrenpoint in County Down and in 1901 Dora was living with her parents and working as a teacher.

Dora was a member of the English WSPU and the secretary of the Northern Branch of the IWSF. In 1913, she was sent to a conference at Caxton Hall in the UK, to discuss the implications of the Cat and Mouse Act with Helen Chenevix. She also spoke at the mass meeting of suffragettes in Hyde Park and explained that Irish suffragettes were coming together under the IWSF's banner, joining women from the north and south, for the cause of suffrage. She also arranged meetings of the IWSF in Newry and Warrenpoint and was active in the Warrenpoint Temperance Society.

Dora regularly wrote for the *Common Cause*, the NUWSS newspaper, about the work of the Ulster suffragists. She was also involved in relief work and acted as secretary for the Suffrage Emergency Council, a group of suffragettes formed to provide support and necessities to those affected by the First World War. Suffragettes were divided on whether the war should be supported or not and Dora wrote to the *Irish Citizen* to explain the position of her society:

The Emergency Meeting of the Federation Executive Committee was held on August 15th. It was then decided the Federation should include among its activities the prevention and relief of distress during the present crisis. The decision was submitted to all the Federated Societies for ratification. This having been obtained, the Federation is now taking an active part in the support of the Suffrage Emergency Council ... Now, for what reasons is the Federation adopt this course? It is perfectly clear that to divert the energies of suffrage workers into other channels may involve a slackening of the ordinary suffrage propaganda: it may be easily urged that this is no moment for such a course. The present crisis supplies the clearest evidence of the urgent need for the enfranchisement of women. Had women been given their fair share in the management of European affairs during the last twenty years the probabilities of this war would have been greatly lessened. The pitiful difficulty experienced by the average 'womanly' woman in finding scope for her energy in the present crisis supplies another argument for the need of that education in citizenship, which the use of the vote can alone afford. Only grave reasons can justify a suffrage organisation in slackening its propaganda for the sake of relief work ...

Our principle justification for undertaking this work was our deep conviction that it is necessary. The question whether the war is justifiable we do not discuss, any more than we discussed the question whether Home Rule was good for the country or bad for the country, I may say in passing, the opinion on the former subject is very strong, but I have no wish to enter into a discussion on it here. The war is here. If the nation is to be saved women must help in the saving. It may be argued that this is only a stronger reason for holding back; the 'difficulty of the Government is the opportunity of the Suffragists'; we ought to refuse all assistance to the Government until we have obtained a pledge for the early introduction of a Government measure enfranchising women. To do otherwise, it may be said, is to haul down the flag of Suffrage first, and hand over our fighting forces to the enemy without conditions.

Our answer is, we cannot do this, because we might destroy the nation ... We are deeply convinced this war will be fought out, not only by the grim lines of guarding ships and thousands of armed men, but by the so-called non-combatants at home. We have always held the argument: 'Women cannot fight, therefore they should not vote' as being worthless ...

For the present our duty is to help to save the nation by lessening its suffering: in the future our duty will be to help to save it by lessening the dangers of another catastrophe as the present. In other words, for the present we will organise relief work: in the future we will again throw our whole energy in the work for votes for women.[1]

The *Irish Citizen* was notoriously anti-war but their editors allowed discussion between suffragettes through the pages of their paper. The war brought about a lot of change, the stopping of militant suffragette activity in particular, as the women who had been involved in the suffrage movement were caught

Irish delegates at a Hyde Park rally. (© Museum of London)

Cat and Mouse act poster. (© Museum of London)

up on which side of the war debate they were on. Some became nurses, others campaigned for peace. Dora believed in relief work and providing assistance through the IWSF.

Little is known of Dora's later years but she moved to Dublin and saw the vote for women become a reality. She died in the Rathdown district in 1950.

Margaret McCoubrey
(1880–1955)

Margaret was born to the Mearns family in 1880 near Glasgow, Scotland. She married into an Irish family around 1906 and moved to Belfast with her husband, John Taylor McCoubrey, who was sixteen years her senior. They were both Presbyterian and settled in Ormeau, County Down.

Margaret began her political career by joining the WSPU and represented the women of the North of Ireland at their meetings in the UK. She was also a member of the IWSS. This society was originally founded as the North of Ireland Women's Suffrage Society in 1873 by Isabella Tod, but changed its name around 1909. Centred in Belfast, it also had branches across the North and Margaret founded the Belfast branch in the city centre.

Margaret canvassed voters on behalf of the IWSS for a Derry by-election with the aim of keeping the liberal candidate out of a seat. The candidate, Mr Hogg, was also a nationalist and her actions did little to endear her to the supporters of nationalism. Margaret was a socialist and agreed with militant tactics, although she was never imprisoned for her actions.

In 1914, after the WSPU had ended their Ulster Campaign, Margaret became the secretary of the IWFL's Ulster Centre. This was a short-lived endeavour but one Margaret gave her time and energy to get off the ground.

The centre sold copies of the *Irish Citizen* and other suffragette newspapers and leaflets, as well as having a library where women could peruse feminist tracts and works of a suffrage nature. Unfortunately, although Margaret had tried to rally new members, the centre was closed in 1915 and suffragette attention was diverted by the First World War.

During this time, Margaret joined the peace movement and in 1917 ran a peace and suffrage campaign in Belfast. She made her position clear in an address she delivered to the Ulster Socialist Party that was consequently published in the *Irish Citizen*, entitled 'The Chivalry of War':

> The time will come when chivalry will mean the care and protection by the strong for all who are weaker either physically or morally. This new conception of chivalry will utterly abolish our existing systems for the maintenance of law and order: our gigantic farce called Courts of Justice, with their unjust administration. In those days there shall be no need for charitable organisations, for prisons, or for rescue homes.
>
> This may seem to you like a dream of a tired present-day socialist. To me it is with equal certainty a vision of the standard which shall exist when women get their chance of wiping false ideas of chivalry forever off the slate – when women get their chance of being men's comrades and equals – not playthings, to be treated indulgently, nor yet economic slaves to be exploited and taken advantage of.
>
> But to leave alone the past and the future, let us consider the present. I want to-night to talk about the chivalry of war – or, perhaps, to be more accurate – the chivalry of the war – as it is not my intention to refer to any but the present war. We have heard much and read much on the questions of Britain's obligations to take part in this great European carnage. Arguments – both pro and con – have not been wanting. But one argument which has not been voiced to the extent it ought to have been, which has not

been considered at all by those superior beings, those Supermen – the diplomats who made the war, but who are not the men found in the front fighting line – is the argument that with anything like a true conception of chivalry, war would not have been declared by any civilised country without first of all consulting the womanhood of that country on the question.

In the past women have always borne part of the weight of war, and the major part. In primitive times women suffered for the destruction of the fields they had tilled and the houses they had built. In more modern times women, in taxes and material loss and additional labour, have borne equally with men the cost of war; and I need hardly refer to what women as nurses have done – since the days of Florence Nightingale until now – to alleviate suffering and pain, and to preserve, if possible, that mysterious force called life which, at times and seasons, men value so lightly. Women's relation to war is so intimate, so personal, so indissoluble, that had chivalry existed at all she must needs have been consulted. Men have made the boomerangs, the maxim guns, the Zeppelins, and the other murderous appliances of modern warfare. Women produce the primal munition of war, without which no other would exist. Women pay the first cost on all human life.

What, think ye, would be the thought of a woman who looked down on a battlefield of slain and wounded? It would not be 'there lie so many Germans, so many British, or so many French'. It would be 'so many mothers' sons! All our service of motherhood gone for naught – that an acre of ground may be manured with human flesh where next year the green grass shall grow and the red poppies gleem redder than before!'

On the day when woman takes her place beside man in the government of affairs, shall be heralded the death of war as a means of settling human differences. In the manhood and womanhood of the future no tinsel of trumpets or flags will seduce into insanity of recklessly destroying life, not gild the wilful taking of life with any other name than that of murder, whether it be the slaughter of the million or of human beings one by one. Not because women lack courage, not because we admit even physical incapacity, not because we assume higher virtues than men, will women declare against war, but solely and simply because women alone appreciate at its highest the value of human life.[1]

In later years, Margaret was made general secretary of the Co-operative Women's Guild and was elected to represent Irish guildswomen on the International Women's Co-operative Committee. Their work included discussing the Criminal Law Act, the Medical treatment of School Children Act, housing reform, sanitation and the need for female constables.

In 1920, she was elected as a Labour MP for the Dock ward of Belfast and became an active member of the Independent Labour Party. She died in 1955.

Afterword

In the course of my research for this book, I have found many names mentioned but very little information about several of the suffragists and suffragettes who contributed to Ireland's fight for the vote for women. There were suffrage societies all around the country and hundreds of women were involved in the struggle, yet their stories are hard to find. I hope this book gives you, the reader, a snapshot of some of the women involved and encourages you to delve deeper into your own family and local history, to find the stories of even more women who fought for the suffrage cause.

The General Prison Board papers are incomplete, with files missing on several of the imprisoned suffragettes including Maud Lloyd, Hilda Webb and Majorie Hasler. There is also very little archive material on Dora Ryan and Annie Walsh. All of these women served prison sentences for their actions. Maud Lloyd, Hilda Webb and Majorie Hasler were imprisoned with Kathleen Houston and received a severe six-month sentences. Dora Ryan and Annie Walsh were convicted with Marguerite Palmer and sentenced to six weeks – all the women had broken glass windows in a statement of militant action to underline their right to vote. Another couple of suffragettes, Gwendoline Martin and Bronwen Portal, were sentenced to four days' imprisonment on the 23 March 1914 for posting a suffrage bill on St Matthias' church. All their file contains is a note taken from the medical officer's journal that states they refused to be medically examined or to take food, but that bread, butter and milk should be available to them at all times and meals offered to them at the usual times. I can find no other information about them but I would like to think that their stories were passed down through their families and maybe one of you will know who these women were and why they chose to become suffragettes.

Being a suffragist or suffragette in Ireland wasn't simple. There was so much more going on. The suffrage movement developed along with the nationalist movement and the rise of the Labour movement. Ireland had its own civil war, fought for its independence and the world had its first global war. All of this combined to makes the times one of huge political upheaval. And the women were caught up in it – divided sometimes, together at others – as they fought for the right to vote against a world, and their own country, in turmoil.

Today, we think little of having the right to vote. It is something that we expect to be able to do, a given right, and many of us don't even use it. For those women fighting for the cause 100 years ago, this would have been unspeakable and unacceptable. They endangered their lives by hunger striking, accepted that they may be force-fed and given criminal convictions for their beliefs because being involved in the male-dominated world of politics was the way in which they saw that their country could change. Having the vote meant everything to them.

I will leave you with one question – what does it mean to you?

Notes

A Note on References

References throughout attributed as NAI/GPB/SFRG refer to the National Archives of Ireland General Prison Board Suffragette Papers and include the name of the suffragette, the date (if given) and the reference number.

The Militant Suffragettes

Margaret Connery

1 NAI/GPB/SFRG/1/4, Margaret Connery, 18 November 1912
2 'The New Force in Irish Politics', *Irish Citizen*, August 1918, cited in Ryan, *Irish Feminism and the Vote*, Folens, 1996

Margaret Cousins

1 J.H. & M.E. Cousins, *We Two Together*, Madras: Ganesh & Co., 1950
2 J.H. & M.E. Cousins, *We Two Together*, Madras: Ganesh & Co., 1950
3 J.H. & M.E. Cousins, *We Two Together*, Madras: Ganesh & Co., 1950
4 NAI/GPB/SFRG/1/5, Margaret Cousins
5 *Irish Independent*, 28 February 1913
6 *Irish Citizen*, 27 July 1912, cited in Ryan, *Irish Feminism and the Vote*, Folens, 1996

Kathleen Emerson

1 'Holloway Jingles', The British Library Board, General Reference Collection 11604.de.29
2 *Irish Citizen*, 1912, cited in Ryan, *Irish Feminism and the Vote*, Folens, 1996
3 NAI/GPB/SFRG/1/4, Kathleen Emerson
4 *Irish Independent*, 21 November 1912

Mabel Purser

1 *Freeman's Journal*, 5 March 1913

Hanna Sheehy Skeffington

1 A.S.S. and R. Owens, *Votes for Women: Irish Women's Struggle for the Vote*, Dublin, 1975
2 NAI/GPB/SFRG/1/1, Hanna Sheehy Skeffington
3 'Message from Mrs Sheehy Skeffington', *Irish Citizen*, 13 December 1913, cited in Ryan, *Irish Feminism and the Vote*, Folens, 1996

Marguerite Palmer

1 *Irish Independent*, 14 June 1913
2 'The Tales of the Tullamore Mice', *Irish Citizen*, 26 July 1913, cited in Ryan, *Irish Feminism and the Vote*, Folens, 1996

The Murphy Sisters

1 NAI/GPB/SFRG/1/1, Margaret Murphy, 5 July 1912
2 NAI/GPB/SFRG/1/1, Margaret Murphy, 24 June 1912
3 NAI/GPB/SFRG/1/1, Margaret Murphy, 15 July 1912
4 *Aberdeen Journal*, 18 July 1913

Barbara Hoskins

1 NAI/GPB/SFRG/1/5, Barbara Hoskins, 7 February 1913

Kathleen Houston

1 *Aberdeen Journal*, 23 November 1910
2 NAI/GPB/SFRG/1/2, Kathleen Houston

The English Suffragettes

1 *Irish Citizen*, 10 August 1912, cited in Ryan, *Irish Feminism and the Vote*, Folens, 1996

The Belfast Suffragettes

1 NAI/GPB/SFRG/1/14, Joan Wickham

The Political Suffragettes

Louie Bennett

1 *Irish Citizen*, January 1918, cited in Ryan, *Irish Feminism and the Vote*, Folens, 1996

Maud Gonne

1 *Irish Citizen*, June & July 1919, cited in Ryan, *Irish Feminism and the Vote*, Folens, 1996

Delia Larkin

1 *Irish Worker*, 1911

Countess Constance de Markievicz

1 *Irish Citizen*, 23 October 1915, cited in Ryan, *Irish Feminism and the Vote*, Folens, 1996

Isabella Tod

1 *Englishwoman's Review*, January 1898

Jennie Wyse-Power

1 *Irish Citizen*, 1912, cited in Ryan, Irish Feminism and the Vote, Folens, 1996
2 *Irish Independent*, 28 May 1914

Marion Duggan

1 *Irish Citizen*, 5 April 1913, cited in Ryan, *Irish Feminism and the Vote*, Folens, 1996
2 *Irish Citizen*, 11 July 1914, cited in Ryan, *Irish Feminism and the Vote*, Folens, 1996

Mary MacSwiney

1 *Irish Citizen*, 2 May 1914, cited in Ryan, *Irish Feminism and the Vote*, Folens, 1996
2 *Irish Citizen*, 23 May 1914, cited in Ryan, *Irish Feminism and the Vote*, Folens, 1996
3 *Irish Citizen*, 23 May 1914, cited in Ryan, *Irish Feminism and the Vote*, Folens, 1996

Susanne Rouviere Day

1 *Irish Citizen*, September 1913, cited in Ryan, *Irish Feminism and the Vote*, Folens, 1996

Dora Mellone

1 'ISF and Relief Work' in *Irish Citizen*, 12 September 1914, cited in Ryan, *Irish Feminism and the Vote*, Folens, 1996

Margaret McCoubrey

1 'The Chivalry of War' in *Irish Citizen*, 27 February 1915, cited in Ryan, *Irish Feminism and the Vote*, Folens, 1996

Bibliography

Christensen Nelson, Carolyn, *Literature of the Women's Suffrage Campaign in England* (Broadview Press: Ontario, 2004)

Conlon, Lil, *Cumann na mBan and the Women of Ireland* (Kilkenny Press: Kilkenny, 1969)

Connolly, Linda, *The Irish Women's Movement from Revolution to Devolution* (The Lilliput Press: Dublin, 2003)

Cousins, James H. and Margaret, E., *We Two Together* (Ganesh & Co: Madras, 1950)

Crawford, Elizabeth, *The Women's Suffrage Movement in Britain and Ireland* (Routledge: London, 2006)

Cullen, Mary and Luddy, Maria, *Female Activists: Irish Women and Change 1900–1960* (The Woodfield Press: Dublin, 2001)

Cullen, Mary and Maria Luddy, *Women, Power and Consciousness in Nineteenth Century Ireland* (Attic Press: Dublin, 1995)

Cullen Owens, Rosemary, *Louie Bennett* (Cork University Press: Cork, 2001)

Cullen Owens, Rosemary, *Smashing Times: A History of the Irish Women's Suffrage Movement* (Attic Press: Dublin, 1984)

Daly, Paul, O'Brien, Ronan and Rouse, Paul, *Making the Difference? The Irish Labour Party 1912–2012* (The Collins Press: Cork, 2012)

Day, Susanne R., *The Amazing Philanthropists* (Sidgwick and Jackson: London, 1916)

Fox, R.M., *Rebel Irish Women* (Talbot Press: Dublin, 1935)

Irish Citizen newspaper, published Dublin 1912–1920

Jeffares, Norman and Macbride White, Anna (eds), *The Autobiography of Maud Gonne: A Servant of the Queen* (The University of Chicago Press: Chicago, 1994)

John, N.A. (ed.), *Holloway Jingles*, written in Holloway Prison during March and April 1912, Glasgow, 1912. By kind permission of the British Library Board. General Reference Collection 11604.de.29

Levenson, Leah and Natterstad, Jerry H., *Hanna Sheehy Skeffington: Irish Feminist* (Syracuse University Press: Syracuse, 1986)

Lewis, Gifford, *Somerville and Ross: The World of the Irish RM* (Penguin: London, 1987)

Luddy, Maria, *Women in Ireland 1800–1918: A Documentary History* (Cork University Press: Cork, 1995)

Matthews, Ann, *Renegades: Irish Republican Women 1900–1922* (Mercier Press: Cork, 2010)

Murphy, Cliona, *The Women's Suffrage Movement and Irish Society in the Early Twentieth Century* (Temple University Press: Philadelphia, 1989)

O'Hogartaigh, Margaret, *Quiet Revolutionaries: Irish Women in Education, Medicine & Sport 1861–1964* (History Press Ireland: Dublin, 2011)

O'Neill, Marie, *From Parnell to De Valera: A Biography of Jennie Wyse Power* (Blackwater Press: Dublin, 1991)

Phillips, Melanie, *The Ascent of Woman* (Abacus: London, 2004)

Rogan, Mary, *Prison Policy in Ireland: Politics, Penal-Welfarism and Political Imprisonment* (Routledge, 2011)

Roper, Esther, *The Prison Letters of Countess Markievicz* (Virago: London, 1987)

Ryan, Louise, *Irish Feminism and the Vote: An Anthology of the Irish Citizen Newspaper 1912–1920* (Folens: Dublin, 1996)

Sheehy Skeffington, A. and Owens, R. (eds), *Votes for Women: Irish Women's Struggle for the Vote* (Dublin, 1975)

Tiernan, Sonja, *Eva Gore-Booth: An Image of Such Politics* (Manchester University Press: Manchester, 2012)

Ward, Margaret, *Maud Gonne: Ireland's Joan of Arc* (Pandora: London, 1990)